Justin Patten is a solicitor and mediator accredited by the Academy of Experts and founded Human Law in 2002. The firm deals a wide range of probate and inheritance issues including executor and trust problems and will validity legal cases.

Justin has also worked for Which?, advising its members on elderly client issues.

AF722589

A Practical Guide to Elderly Law

2nd Edition

A Practical Guide to Elderly Law

2nd Edition

Justin Patten, BA Hon, CPE
Solicitor, Accredited Mediator and
Principal at Human Law LLP

Law Brief Publishing

Published 2021 by Law Brief Publishing, an imprint of Law Brief Publishing Ltd
30 The Parks
Minehead
Somerset
TA24 8BT

www.lawbriefpublishing.com

Paperback: 978-1-913715-84-7

To Bella and Rommey

PREFACE

The Second Edition of this book continues to provide an accessible read for lawyers and people interested in the area of elderly law. It reflects the updated law including recent cases and the new edition adds another chapter on Executors and how to effectively remove them together with more detail on the area of Trusts, probate fraud and undue influence. The book provides a number of practical tips to ensure that people are able to successfully navigate the complex and often demanding legal processes within this growing area of the law. It also covers other key topics including Will Validity, Inheritance Law, Lasting Power of Attorney, Mediation (both law and practice) and Mental Capacity, including the Court of Protection.

This book reflects the law as of 1st March 2021.

I would like to thank you my publishers Tim Kevan and Garry Wright for their support and enabling the second edition to happen.

Justin Patten
March 2021

CONTENTS

CHAPTER ONE

WILL VALIDITY

Assessing the Validity of the Will & the Practice

What are the proper formalities of the will?

Age

As a general rule, a testator must have reached the age of 18 at the time of making a Will (the Wills Act 1837, s.7).

Formalities

In addition, for deaths arising after 1 January 1983, Section 9 of the Wills Act 1837 (as substituted by the Administration of Justice Act 1982, s. 17) ('the Act') says that no Will is valid unless:

- It is in writing, and signed by the Testator, or by some other person in his presence and by his direction; and
- It appears that the Testator intended by his signature to give effect to the Will; and
- The signature is made or acknowledged by the Testator in the presence of two or more witnesses present at the same time; and
- Each witness either:
    - attests and signs the Will.
    - or acknowledges his signature, in the presence of the Testator (but not normally in the presence of any other witnesses), but no form of attestation shall be necessary.

In the event these formalities are not complied with the will reverts to intestacy.

TIP

With respect to validity disputes, check carefully the will once you get your hands on it. Every aspect such as the typeface, date, attestation clauses.

What Is Intestacy?

In the event that the will is invalid you will either be left with the previous will or the rules of intestacy will apply.

What are the rules of intestacy?

When a person dies without leaving a valid will, their property (the estate) must be shared out according to certain rules. These are called the rules of intestacy. A person who dies without leaving a will is called an intestate person. Please see Appendix 1 for more details of intestacy. Also consider government rules https://www.gov.uk/inherits-someone-dies-without-will

What is the form of the signature?

The signature of the testator can be merely a mark (for example a thumb prints as in Borman v Lel)

Can Someone Below 18 Make a Valid Will?

Not unless they have privileged access.

Section 11 of the WA states the formal requirements do not apply to:

Any soldier being in actual military service, or any mariner or seaman at sea… though under the age of eighteen years.

Where Does the Will Have to Be Signed?

It does not have to be "at the foot or end thereof" (following the AJA 1982 s 17).

It can be signed by someone other than the testator as it or her direction.

Who Can Prepare a Will?

Anyone can prepare a will.

Nevertheless, suspicion will be raised if the person who prepares it is:

- A major beneficiary
- A close relative of a major beneficiary
- A partner of a major beneficiary

There is no rule that prohibits one of the above preparing the will, but suspicions will be raised.

What Mental Capacity Do You Have to Have to Make a Will?

The common law standard was laid down in Banks v Goodfellow and remains the leading case which is that the testator must:

a) Understand the nature of his act (sound mind) that is he is making a will and its effects?

b) Understand the extent of his property being disposed of (sound memory) though he/she does not need remember every one of his assets.

c) Be able to comprehend and appreciate the claims to which a person making a will ought to give effect (sound understanding)

Consider the Interplay with the Mental Capacity Act 2005 (MCA)

Overall, it is still unclear as to the Mental Capacity Act 2005 (MCA) which came into force on 1st October 2007 as to the impact upon mental capacity.

The Courts have not given clear guidance as to what extent the MCA applies to the issue of testamentary capacity.

In Scammell v Farmer the Deputy High Court Judge ruled against the application of the MCA because the case was not within the "purposes of the Act" and secondly, because the relevant will had been made before the Act came into force.

Judicial ambiguity rules since this point so the key is to focus on the common law legislation in formulating your client's case.

Was the Golden Rule Applicable and if So, Was It Applied?

What Are the Key Duties of Legal Practitioners?

If a will has been prepared by a solicitor, it creates additional obligations upon them.

The Golden Rule

The 'Golden Rule' was set out in the judgment of Templeman J in Kenward v. Adams (1975) The Times 29 Nov:

> "*In the case of an aged testator or a testator who has suffered a serious illness, there is one golden rule which should always be observed, however straightforward matters may appear, and however difficult or tactless it may be to suggest that precautions be taken: the making of a will by such a testator ought to be witnessed or approved by a medical practitioner who satisfies himself of the capacity and understanding of the testator, and records and preserves his examination and finding*".

While the golden rule has been widely approved by the Courts as having the potential to reduce the risk of a claim of lack of testamentary capacity (e.g., see Sharp v. Adam), and should therefore be offered to testators as an additional precaution even if not observed.

The rule is expressed to apply to two categories of testator, namely those who are 'aged' or have suffered a 'serious illness', and therefore the next step is to consider which illnesses are 'serious' for this purpose, and how old 'aged' is.

The case of Re Simpson [1977] 121 SJ 224 provides that there is one golden rule that is to be observed, however straightforward the will and however tactless the suggestion, that the making of a will by an aged or seriously ill testator ought to be witnessed or approved by a medical practitioner who has satisfied himself of the capacity and understanding of the testator, and records and preserves his examination or findings.

Will GP Evidence Suffice to Prevent a Successful Validity Claim?

If it is assessed that medical evidence is appropriate in the circumstances then the initial point of contact would be someone who knows the client, most often their GP. However, the suggestion that a GP assessment will suffice has been met with some criticism. It has been suggested that, in order for the golden rule to have substance, a specialist should be approached.

On the other hand, the associated cost, delay and apprehension that can be felt by a client in seeking further specialist advice can potentially cause an adverse reaction.

What Is the Burden of Proof?

The common law rules regarding burden of proof concerning testamentary capacity are set out in Key v Key (2010):

a) While the burden starts with the propounder of a will to establish capacity, where the will is duly executed and appears rational on its face then the court will presume capacity.

b) In such a case the evidential burden then shifts to the objector to raise a real doubt about capacity.

c) If a real doubt is raised, the evidential burden shifts back to the propounder to establish capacity, nevertheless.

Provided the testator had testamentary capacity at the time the will was signed and witnessed it may not matter if the testator loses full capacity. Generally, the time to test whether capacity existed is the time of execution of the will. However, the dates and still valid case of Parker v Felgate confirms that, in limited and defined circumstances, a Will can still be valid, even if the testator loses capacity between giving instructions and signing the Will. As long as T had capacity when giving instructions, Parker v Felgate confirms that a much lower degree of understanding is necessary when the Will is signed. A recent case of Clancy v Clancy (2003) shows that this is good law.

Knowledge and Approval

The testator must know and approve the contents of the will (this is not applicable to a statutory will).

The legal test is that the testator must know and approve the contents of the will at the time of execution.

In all cases, however, and irrespective of age, it is necessary to provide clients with proper advice and to assess whether it is necessary to obtain medical evidence.

Further, a client should be advised that, in the event of a subsequent challenge to their will on the basis of lack of capacity, a lack of contemporaneous medical opinion may make the challenge more likely to succeed.

Case: Brennan – v – Prior 2013] EWHC 287(ch)

The case of Brennan v Prior provides a useful illustration of how the Courts assess claims that a testator lacked knowledge of, or did not approve, the contents of his or her Will.

To admit a Will to proof, the court must be satisfied that the testator understood what he was doing and its effect so that the document represents his testamentary intentions. It is for the party seeking to propound the Will to show that the testator understood his Will.

Where a Will was executed in accordance with the formalities set out in section 9 of the Wills Act 1837 by a person with testamentary capacity there is usually a presumption the testator knew and approved its contents.

In addition, a "very strong" presumption exists where the Will was prepared by a solicitor and read over to the testator before execution.

A party seeking to propound a Will may not be able to rely simply on due execution and capacity where the circumstances surrounding its preparation or execution "excite the suspicion of the Court" – where the Will was drafted by a person who benefits under it or contains complex provisions which the testator was unlikely to understand.

A party seeking successfully to challenge a Will must produce evidence of circumstances which leaves the Court not satisfied that, on the balance of probabilities, the testator understood its nature and effect, and sanctioned the dispositions it made.

As a matter of policy, the Court is cautious about accepting such challenges. Wills frequently give rise to feelings of disappointment for would-be beneficiaries which can lead to contentions that the Will did not reflect the testator's true wishes. If judges were too ready to accept such contentions the principle of testamentary freedom could be undermined.

Given this it is critical that the lawyer is satisfied that there is strong evidence to show an absence of knowledge and approval from the testator.[1]

Undue Influence & Persuasion

Sir James Hannen further defined undue influence in the context of probate in Wingrove v Wingrove (1885) as being "To be undue influence in the eye of the law there must be – to sum it up in one word – coercion".

---

1 Some useful summaries of the law – https://www.thegazette.co.uk/all-notices/content/103463

The case of Brennan v Prior & Others [2013] EWHC 287(ch) illustrated that persuasion was due influence in which Ms Brennan challenged the will alleging undue influence by the siblings. However, dismissing Ms Brennan's challenge, the judge said that evidence did not support her accusations of dishonesty; there was nothing irrational about the testator's bequests, and that while there 'is plenty of evidence that [his sisters] had the opportunity to influence [the testator] in the making of his will...I find persuasion but not coercion.'

Presumption of Due Execution

In the case of Channon v Perkins [2]it was aid that where the will had a full and valid attestation clause and represented the deceased's wishes, there must be cogent and clear evidence, i.e., testimony which constitutes 'the strongest evidence', to overturn a will.

What Are the Pre-Court Steps to Take?

Due to the expense of going to Court as solicitors you need to be careful prior to commencing legal proceedings.

Ultimately the ability to challenge a will is dependent on a series of variables which focus on assessing the evidence?

- Get the will & review it. To attack the validity of the will you need to obtain the will – If a person refused to provide the will an application can be made for the issue of a witness summons via the Senior Courts Act. It is important to scrutinise it and check as you see the formalities have been complied with.

- Is it handwritten or not? If a beneficiary handwrote the will then this will evidence that will raise suspicion.

- Is It Consistent? If a significant beneficiary handwrote the will the

[2] https://www.casemine.com/judgement/uk/5a8ff7a760d03e7f57eb0d6f

more likely it is to be attacked later.

- How complex is the will? The more complicated it is the more likely that it can be attacked for lack of knowledge and approval particularly if there are doubts over the mental capacity of the testator.

- Who were the attesting witnesses? Could they have been in any way influenced? (An approach can be made to the attesting witnesses regarding the deceased's state of mind

- How was the will executed?

- What about the signature? Does this match the testator's signature on other documents? Was it shaky?

- Has the deceased made a previous will? If so, was there a significant change on the previous will? Does anyone benefit in a different file?

2. Get the will file if a solicitor has been instructed. This will include all the documents and can be done via a Larke v Nugus letter.

What Is the Point of a Larke v Nugus Letter?[3]

In the case of Larke v Nugus, the Court of Appeal refused to order those challenging the will to pay the costs of the challenge even though the will was found to be valid. This was because the solicitor who had prepared the will refused to make information available at an early stage which, had it been given, could have prevented a full trial.

The purpose of a Larke v Nugus letter is to prevent money being spent on litigation by the provision of early legal disclosure and to reveal evidence which can be key to probate dispute. The onus is on the receiving solicitor to provide a prompt reply and relevant evidence to facilitate early settlement. Thus, the solicitor should provide a full response to a request within a reasonable period, for example: two to three weeks and provide

---

[3] More information is provided here: https://www.thegazette.co.uk/all-notices/content/101713

key parts of the will file.

What is The Content of Such a Letter?

The form is an effective question process which will include such questions as how long the Solicitor had known the deceased, the date the Solicitor received instructions from the deceased, notes of all meetings and telephone calls, including confirmation of where the meeting took place and who else was present at the meeting. All relevant if you have concerns over the validity of will.

How Useful Are They?

Often, very. It will often indicate whether the Solicitor correctly advised the deceased, whether there were individuals present at instruction/execution to support allegations of undue influence and whether the Solicitor undertook the correct test for testamentary capacity. Can reveal a crucial evidential point. If you are going to attack an aspect of the will making process this is where you must go.

3. Assess Medical Evidence

The Access to Health Records Act 1990 s 3(1) (f) provides that an application for access to health records may be made by "the patient's personal representative and any person who may have a claim arising out of the patient's death." If medical records suggest a loss of capacity, one can request a retrospective report.

Legal Proceedings

Validity disputes are brought about in the Chancery Division of the High Court CPR Practice Division 7A sets out the rules deciding whether proceedings should be commenced in the High Court or County Court.

Generally, £25,000 is the lower limit for issuing any non-personal injury case in the High Court.

https://formfinder.hmctsformfinder.justice.gov.uk/n1-eng.pdf

Probate Claims follow the CPR Part 7 procedure but are modified in the following ways:

- The time limit for acknowledging service is 28 days after service of the particulars of claim.
- The time limit for filing the defence is also 28 days after service of the particulars of claim.

Once the action has started the relevant Court will contact Leeds District Probate Registry asking that all testamentary documents, grants of probate and any other relevant documents are sent to the relevant office.

Limitation Period

There is no specific limitation period in probate claims although the defences of laches and acquiescence apply.

Other Parties

Those who are entitled under the will at issue or a previous will or on intestacy together with anyone claiming entitlement to administer the estate as Personal Representative should be joined as a party to the action.

The relevant court rules in helping to make this decision are:

CPR r 19.6 to 19.8a

The claim form should be served within 4 months of issue.

Pre-Action Protocol

There is no specific protocol for validity disputes but parties in order to comply with this need to exchange as much as information as possible to allow themselves to understand the side's position as much as possible.

Make appropriate attempts to resolve the case by ADR if possible.

In addition, practitioners should comply with the ACTAPS Practice Guidance Notes.

- recommending and providing a precedent for a letter of claim encompassing and adaptable to various types of dispute or claim (e.g., Inheritance Act claims)

- by providing lists of evidential documents to be produced in different types of disputes

- by promoting the early production of medical and social security records and evidence and providing precedent letters to that end (including a letter to a testator's GP agreed with the BMA)

- by providing for early production of evidence of testamentary capacity and a precedent Lark -v- Nugus letter to the testator's solicitor

- by suggesting reasonable time limits

- by providing for cooperation in obtaining joint and third-party letters of authority to disclose evidence

- by reproducing the new CPR covering the representation of unborn, minor, unascertained and incapable parties

- by encouraging mediation on the footing that the outcome will be subject to the approval of the Court in those cases where such approval is indispensable, and

- by providing for those cases where Revenue considerations arise.

If matters are not moving forwards, issue a 21-day letter before action.

TIP

When you are getting into the realms of threating legal action, think carefully about your correspondence not just in terms of showing the legal flaws of the other side's case but more about how to influence the other side.

Judgement in default cannot be obtained for probate claims.

Once a case has been started under CPR 57.11 the case cannot be discontinued.

APPENDIX 1

What is the order of the beneficiaries according to the rules of intestacy?

The order of priority on intestacy is set out in Section 46 of the Administration of Estates Act 1925 (AEA 1925), as amended. The rules in relation to a surviving spouse also changed significantly following the Inheritance and Trustees' Powers Act 2014 (ITPA 2014).

Distributing the estate according to intestacy rules

After you have paid the debts and taxes, you have to distribute the estate according to the intestacy rules.

The surviving husband, wife or civil partner who was still legally married to the deceased can inherit the estate.

The deceased's children might also inherit part of the estate if it's worth more than a certain amount.

Close relatives such as surviving parents or siblings of the deceased could also inherit the estate in certain situations.

Each country has a different rule for working out who gets what and how much.

For more details on working out how to distribute the estate according to the intestacy rules, tool on GOV.UK website.

In England and Wales

If the estate is worth less than £270,000, the spouse will inherit the entire estate.

But if the estate is worth more than £270,000 and there are children:

- the spouse inherits up to £270,000 worth of assets, all the deceased's personal possessions, half of the remainder of the estate.

- the other half is divided equally between the children.

If any child is under the age of 18 when the person died, his or her share is held in statutory trust.

He or she will receive their inheritance when they reach the age of 18, or when they marry or enter into a civil partnership, whichever comes first.

CHAPTER TWO

INHERITANCE CLAIMS

What Makes a Successful Inheritance Claim?

Historically testators in England and Wales have testamentary freedom but as we see below certain categories of persons can make a claim on the estate as laid down in the Inheritance (Provision for Family and Dependants Act) 1975 as amended by other legislation. [4]

TIP

There is no silver bullet to preventing inheritance claims but if you are acting for someone who you/the Testator who is making a will and fear that a claim could be made against the estate consider some of these options to minimise the prospects of a claim:

1. Writing a letter of wishes explaining why X (the person who you do not wish to receive an inheritance) has not been included in the will – the Court would consider this though can be an inflammatory document so be careful in doing this.

2. Providing a legacy but making it a conditional legacy upon X agreeing not to sue.

3. Considering in depth the possibility of X suing and the executors being fully prepared for this eventuality. This will assist the executors and can act as a source of support as they grapple with a disgruntled potential Claimant.

Remember – the key is to minimise the prospects of a successful and/or costly litigation and to be proactive in achieving these goals.
In addition, do not be over-cute. It is not possible to diminish an estate

[4] Law Reform (Succession) Act 1995, Civil Partnership Act 2004, Inheritance, and Trustee Powers Act 2014.

so that no claim can be made against it. If a person diverts money from an estate with the goal of trying to prevent an award under the IPFDA 1975, the Court is able to order that those monies are brought back into the estate.

Who is Eligible to Make a Claim?

The persons eligible to make a claim emerge from s1(1) of IPFDA 1975.

To make a successful claim:

The Deceased must be domiciled in England and Wales and be one of the categories of litigant.

Where after the commencement of this Act a person **dies domiciled in England and Wales** and is survived by any of the following persons: — **And must be in one of the categories below:**

(a) the spouse or civil partner of the deceased;[5]

(b) a former spouse or former civil partner of the deceased, but not one who has formed a[3] subsequent marriage or civil partnership;

(ba) for deaths occurring on after 1st January 1996 any person who, during the whole of the period of two years ending immediately before the date when the deceased died, was living:

i) in the same household as the deceased, and

ii) as the husband or wife or civil; partner of the deceased

(c) a child of the deceased;[6]

---

[5] When focusing on the rights of the spouse to make a claim look at section 3(2) of the Act which provides the guidelines namely the age of the applicant, duration of the marriage/civil partnership, financial and other contributions to the welfare of the family and provision expected on termination of civil partnership/divorce. Some cases worth looking at include – Adams v Lewis 2001 WLR 495, White v White 2001 (http://www.bailii.org/uk/cases/UKHL/2000/54.html).

[6] Historically able-bodied Claimants have struggled to make claims – Re Coventry

d) any person (not being a child of the deceased) who in relation to any marriage or civil partnership to which the deceased was at any time a party, or otherwise in relation to any family in which the deceased at any time stood in the role of a parent, was treated by the deceased as a child of the family;

e) any person (not being a person included in the foregoing paragraphs of this subsection) who immediately before the death of the deceased was being maintained, either wholly or partly, by the deceased;

What is the Court's Approach?

The approach of the Court is in an objective test with two stages:

1. Whether reasonable financial provision has been made for the applicant by the deceased under the will (or through the intestacy rules);

2. If the Court finds that reasonable provision has not been made, it then considers what, it any provision should be made.[7]

The decision is based on facts known at time of application and not time of death.

Has There Been Reasonable Financial Provision for the Would-Be Claimant?

Where Was the Deceased Domiciled?

You need to look at the status of the applicant to determine if there has been reasonable financial provision or not.

Section 1 of the Act makes clear that the 1975 Act only applies to estates at the time of death where deceased was domiciled in England and Wales. The Court needs to look at to see whether deceased retained domicile of

1980 Ch 461 but Ilott v Mitson has shifted goalposts to some extent.

7 This two-fold approach has been confirmed in Robinson v Bird And Another 2003 WTLR 529.

origin. Please look at Cyganik v Agulian 2006 EWCA Civ 129 and Holiday v Musa EWCA 335. The fact nature of deciding domicile makes it hard to predict so if this an issue consider with care.

There are two standards

A key component of the IPFDA and related legislation is the fact that there are **two** standards of provision – In the case of a spouse/civil partner, (including a former spouse or civil partner at the court's discretion) the IPFDA makes a higher standard of provision based on what is reasonable in all the circumstances "whether that provision is required for his or her maintenance" (section 1(2) a. This is termed the spouse standard.

In the case of other categories, they are entitled to what is known as reasonable provision for their maintenance only.

For all applicants, what is reasonable provision?

Matters to which court is to have regard in determining if reasonable are:

- the financial resources and financial needs which the applicant has or is likely to have in the near future;
- the financial resources and financial needs which any other applicant for an order under section 2 of this Act has or is likely to have in the foreseeable future;
- the financial resources and financial needs which any beneficiary of the estate of the deceased has or is likely to have in the foreseeable future;
- any obligations and responsibilities which the deceased had towards any applicant for an order under the said section 2 or towards any beneficiary of the estate of the deceased;
- the size and nature of the net estate of the deceased;

- any physical or mental disability of any applicant for an order under the said section 2 or any beneficiary of the estate of the deceased;
- any other matter, including the conduct of the applicant or any other person, which in the circumstances of the case the court may consider relevant.

Spouse/Civil Partner

In the case of an application made by subsection (1)(a) above by the husband or wife of the deceased (except where the marriage with the deceased was the subject of a decree of judicial separation and at the date of death the decree was in force and the separation was continuing), means such financial provision as it would be reasonable in all the circumstances of the case for a husband or wife to receive, whether that provision is required for his or her maintenance;

In Section 3(2) there are additional guidelines.

The court shall, in addition to the matters specifically mentioned in paragraphs (a) to (f) of that subsection, have regard to—

- the ages of the applicant and the duration of the marriage [or civil partnership];
- the contribution made by the applicant to the welfare of the family of the deceased, including any contribution made by looking after the home or caring for the family.

The Court is required to consider the provision that the applicant might reasonably have expected to receive if, on the day the deceased died, the marriage had not been terminated by death but rather by divorce/dissolution. (The divorce hypothesis)

To be within a s1(1) of the Act, the applicant's marriage must be recognised by laws of England and Wales or by the jurisdictions in which the marriage takes place.

Under the Civil Partnership Act 2004 the Court has power to treat registered same sex couples in the same way as married couples for the purposes of the 1975 Act.

Former Spouse Rights

S 19(b) states that a spouse /c-p whose marriage to deceased has dissolved can apply for provision provided he or she has not remarried.

If she or he remarries subsequently the claim will be limited to one of maintenance between date of death and remarriage.

Other Categories

Reasonable financial provision is limited to what is "reasonable in all circumstances for the applicant to receive for his maintenance"

The courts have a wide discretion when considering what represents reasonable. In Re Coventry 1979 3 WLR "above the breadline" was reasonable and re R E decd 1966 1 WLR "sufficiently to enable the dependant to live neither luxuriously nor miserably, but decently and comfortably according to his or her station in life."

Cohabitee[8] [9]

Where an application for an order under section 2 of this Act is made by virtue of section 1(1) (ba) of this Act, the court shall, in addition to the matters specifically mentioned in paragraphs (a) to (f) of that subsection, have regard to—

---

8 To qualify as a cohabitee, it is necessary for the claimant to have been living with the deceased in the same household during the whole 2 years immediately prior to death.

9 A key case on cohabitees is set out in Re Watson deceased 1999 1FLR 878 -The test of whether the Claimant was living as husband, wife or civil partner is made clear here. A sexual relationship is not necessary to have be classed as a cohabitee. Furthermore, in Patel v Vigh 2013 the fact that the deceased had spent the last two months of her life in hospital did not stop the fact that her and husband had lived in the same household as spouses "during the whole period of two years ending immediately before the date when the deceased died."

- the age of the applicant and the length of the period during which the applicant lived as the husband or wife or civil partner] of the deceased and in the same household as the deceased;

- the contribution made by the applicant to the welfare of the family of the deceased, including any contribution made by looking after the home or caring for the family.

Child of Deceased

This class of potential Claimant includes minors, illegitimate children and adopted children. It does not include a natural child who has been adopted by others.

the court shall, in addition to the matters specifically mentioned in paragraphs (a) to (f) of that subsection, have regard to the manner in which the applicant was being or in which he might expect to be educated or trained, and where the application is made by virtue of section 1(1)(d) the court shall also have regard—

- to whether the deceased maintained the applicant and, if so, to the length of time for which and basis on which the deceased did so, and to the extent of the contribution made by way of maintenance;

- to whether and, if so, to what extent the deceased assumed responsibility for the maintenance of the applicant;]

- to whether in maintaining or assuming responsibility for maintaining the applicant the deceased did so knowing that the applicant was not his own child;

- to the liability of any other person to maintain the applicant

Any person who immediately before the death of the deceased was being maintained by the deceased "otherwise than for full valuable consideration, was making a substantial contribution in money or money's worth towards the reasonable needs of that person."[10]

Section 1(3) of the Act sets out the definition of being maintained for the purposes of s1(1) (e)

What Orders Can The Court Make?

If the Court decides to make an order this can be done in the form of:

- Periodic payments
- A lump sum
- A settlement
- The acquisition of property
- The variation of an existing settlement

In addition, the Court has a new power to vary for the applicant's benefit, the trusts on which the deceased's estate is held (whether under a will or an intestacy – section 2 IPFDA 1975 as amended by paragraph 4, Schedule 2 IPTA 2014.) Before 1 October 2014 the Court only had ancillary power to vary trusts.

Ilott Case[11] – Partial Move to Minimise Confusion

The Ilott case has been one of the most important IFDA cases in the past ten years and it has focused on the ability of particularly children to make successful claims.

---

[10] Some good case law on this area is in re Beaumont (1980) Ch 444 The words in the section 'immediately before' in the context of the maintenance of the claimant by the deceased before the death, were not to be construed literally. The situation was to be viewed as the general arrangements for maintenance in place at the time of the death. In this case a short stay in hospital prior to death is not sufficient to prevent the claim.

[11] https://www.supremecourt.uk/cases/uksc-2015-0203.html

Where Ilott particularly shocked lawyers was that historically adults who were not being maintained by their adult parents were unlikely to be able to make successful claims. Ilott changed this perspective.

The facts were that an estranged adult daughter was estranged from her mother. Because of their estrangement the deceased deliberately and expressly (by her letter of wishes) excluded her daughter from any benefit under her will and chose to leave her estate, worth around £486,000, to three animal charities with which she had no connection during her life.

In Court Mrs Ilott was ostensibly successful. It was held that her mother's will failed to make reasonable financial provision for her and she was awarded a lump sum of £50,000.

Mrs Ilott appealed this decision of the District Judge saying that the award was not enough as it would: deprive her of her means tested state benefits not provide her with sufficient funds with which to buy the housing association property she lived in.

The Court of Appeal set aside the decision. Mrs Illott was awarded £143,000 to allow her to buy her home, together with a further £20,000 for additional income. This was then appealed to the Supreme Court.

Almost 10 years after the first instance decision, the Supreme Court reinstated Mrs Ilott's original £50,000 award.

The significance of the Supreme Court's decision is that the Court of Appeal was wrong to interfere with and increase the award granted by the District Judge. The judge had to make a value judgment based upon the evidence in front of him and he was perfectly entitled to reach the conclusion which he did.

Therefore, the writer believes it will be more difficult to overturn of an initial Court decision.

This is the first occasion that the Supreme Court has been asked to consider a claim under the 1975 Act but he impact for testators – This Case Reinforces the Lack of Clarity of the Law

This area of law raises questions regarding testamentary freedom to dispose of their property as the wish and there is little guidance on how the courts should make this decision.[12]

Lady Hale's judgment sums it up and refers to the law in this area as:

> *"unsatisfactory... giving as it does no guidance as to the factors to be considered in deciding whether an adult child is deserving or undeserving of reasonable maintenance.... The problem with the present law is that it gives virtually no help in deciding how to evaluate these or balance them with other claims on the estate."*

At one level we have a legal vacuum but the position may be overstated and it is important to look at the cases post Ilott.

What has been the Courts approach post Ilott?

Delaforte v Flood [2019].

The Claimant made a claim from the estate of her late grandmother who suffered with dementia as she had given up her career as a ballet dancer to care for her, providing full time care at least six days a week. She took the state benefits that they received as a family and £100 per month. Thus she was remunerated but that payment fell far short of a market rate what she could have earned in her own profession. The Claimant sought an award simply to support her for three years to allow her time to establish a business as a dance teacher. The Claimant's mother and uncle obtained the estate under the terms of the will. While her mother supported her claim, her uncle, defended the claim on the basis she had been paid for what she had done, and they had a commercial arrangement. The outcome was the Claimant won and received an award of £110,000 from an estate of £650,000. In this case the Judge observed 'That is not a reward

[12] Testamentary freedom – the right to leave our assets to whomever we choose – is often quoted as being a fundamental and enshrined principle of succession in England and Wales. There is no 'right to inherit' property from parents or relatives. For a claim to be successful, there must be some good reason for the Court to make an award beyond, for example, the mere fact of a blood relationship: "some reason why it can be said that, in the circumstances, it is unreasonable that no or no greater provision was in fact made." (In re Coventry (1980) Ch 461).

for her plainly meritorious conduct in caring devotedly for her grandmother.... simply represents reasonable financial provision for her maintenance.'

Wellesley v Wellesley & Ors [2019][13]

However, the result was different in this case where the High Court dismissed a claim by the estranged daughter of the 7th Earl Cowley against his £1.3M estate. She received £20,000 from his estate under the terms of his will with the remainder going into trust to provide for his fourth wife and various other family members including his son and step-children. The Court decided that the £20,000 the daughter received was reasonable financial provision as she could otherwise live within her own means (which included the availability to her of state benefit provision). Lady Tara Wellesley had been estranged from her father for 30 years; she sought to argue that this was due to her step-mother forcing her out of the family but the judge held it was in fact down to her disruptive behaviour and a lifestyle of 'drink drugs and bohemia'. She also sought to advance human rights arguments which were simply dismissed. The Deputy Master dismissed her claim that reasonable financial provision should have been in the hundreds of thousands. Central to his decision were his conclusions that the Claimant could support herself financially and she was responsible for the estrangement from her father.

The Deputy Master disregarded any sums claimed relating to the Claimant's disabled son, concluding that there was no evidence that she had any financial responsibility for him. He also disallowed the costs of artist's studio space, since he agreed with the submission that this would not enable her to improve her financial position. He therefore held that she could support herself financially as her income, albeit small, exceeded her outgoings.

The conclusions of the Deputy Master on financial needs and estrangement potentially act as a warning to Claimants. The court will be willing to take a tough stance and dismiss the claim of an impecunious adult child if his or her needs are ill-defined or if the factual evidence points

[13] Wellesley v Wellesley & Ors [2019] EWHC 11 (Ch)

towards the conclusion that the provision was reasonable.

Conclusions

Fundamentally when you have an open legal framework like this the key for the parties (e.g. the testator pre-death), the executors (post death) and the applicant and his or her lawyers (pre and post-death) is to manage their conduct and make sure that all their steps appear reasonable and good after the event, as a judge is going to scrutinise everyone's conduct carefully and must make a value judgment on the case balancing all the needs of the parties.

Specifically, this means for example – the testator perhaps being more inclined to make provisions in the will to the estranged child on the basis the would-be Claimant does not contest the will/ the applicant's being more assertive in seeking to mediate cases/show the closeness of his/her relationship to the deceased while alive/make sensible and possibly open (not without prejudice) offers. Essentially conducting the (would be) litigation even prior to death is critical and more omnipotent than before.

The Supreme Court's decision has been described as a win for testamentary freedom but, the door remains open for 1975 Act claims and in the right circumstances, claims by adult children will still succeed.

Cases of this kind are very fact specific and as a lawyer it is important not to get too absorbed with the client's own position but rather to always maintain the overall big picture as money to be distributed is not unlimited. I pay particular attention to the character of the parties and evaluate how they will come across in the heat of litigation.

Practical Steps

Evidential Checks

If you are acting on behalf of a potential Claimant consider making a series of checks on the evidence and be ruthless in assessing the financial worth of the claim.

Also, remember a 1975 Act claim is not a challenge to the validity of the will. A caveat can be a useful step in blocking the probate and protecting funds but if that caveat is challenged it will need to be withdrawn to minimise risks on costs.

Indeed, if you lodge a caveat on erroneous grounds there is legal exposure.

A standing search is a sensible move to see if a grant has been issued and if note you can be notified once this happened.[14]

TIP – IPFDA Claims

One of the crucial aspects of the IPFA Claim is the ability to link or (unlink) if acting for the Executors between the parties.

Claims under this legislation rely on a witness statement being issued with the Claim form so you need to frontload your evidence.

Given this, as the lawyer you want to have a thorough overview of the documents which can include the following:

(a) Death Certificate

(b) Grant of Probate/letters of administration

(c) Will/former wills

(d) Letter of Wishes/Any relevant correspondence on will making intentions

(e) Birth Certificates

(f) Bank Statements/Credit Card Statements of both deceased and applicants

(g) Photographic/Email evidence of relationship

---

[14] https://www.gov.uk/wills-probate-inheritance/searching-for-probate-records

(h) Evidence of Applicants – debts/financial needs

(i) Evidence of Applicant Earnings

(j) Photographs, Cards – Evidence of Applicant Linking to Deceased/ Evidence of Deceased Linking to Non-Applicant

TIP – Financial Assessment

At this level, it comes down to emotion and money.

It is critical at an early stage to assess the size and nature of the estate and whether it is worthwhile for either party to make/resist a claim.

Fundamentally, a key question to ask – Is there enough in the estate for the amount obtained/given to exceed legal costs in obtaining that provision. Ultimately an estate which can appear significant can be undermined by debt, Inheritance tax liability and/or high administration expenses.

Ultimately is it worth litigating about?

It is better to ask these questions at an early stage rather than at a later stage.

The Executor should go through this process and should have no hesitation in communicating the lack of money within the estate if he she thinks there is.

Conversely if acting for the Claimant, focus on the following documents to try to see how much is within the estate:

Obtain a Copy of the grant – (this shows the size of the estate)

Ask from the Executors – Evidence of Assets, whether the deceased held property.

Joint Property

The court's view of property which is within joint tenancy is governed by s 9 of IPFDA 1975 (as amended by paragraph 7 of Schedule 3 to the IPTA 2014).

Section 9 permits the Court to treat the deceased's share of this property as part of the deceased's net estate to such an extent as the Court considers to be just and equitable.

Section 9 Time Limit

Please note that if an application is to be made under s 9 of the Act requesting the court treat the deceased's several joint tenancies as part of the net estate must be made within 6 months of date of the grant. There is no ability of the Court to extend the time limit.

Right to Claim is Personal

Where an applicant dies before any order is made, the executor is not able to carry on the action for the benefit of the estate.[15]

TIP – Be Conservative on Distribution

Whilst, in accordance with pre-action protocol arrangements, applicants should engage in correspondence with the executors and/or beneficiaries of the estate prior to bringing proceedings, this does not always happen, so the estate may be unaware of a claim until it is served.

What about where the executor is on notice of a potential claim but this has not been issued within six months (or longer) of the date of the grant?

In this situation, it would be sensible t for the executor to give the intended claimant notice of any proposed distribution of the estate. If in doubt about whether the estate should be distributed, the executor can

[15] Whyte v Ticehurst 1986 2 All ER 158

seek directions from the court under Part 64 of the Civil Procedure Rules.

Delayed Distribution

Executors should not distribute estates for at least six months from the date of issue of the grant (apart from paying out small legacies, which it will often be appropriate to do). This is because potential applicants have six months from the date of the grant in which to issue proceedings under the 1975 Act.

Executors who wait for six months from the date of the grant before distributing the estate are granted protection from liability, under the 1975 Act.

Indeed executors should, in fact, wait for 10 months from the date of the grant before distributing the estate, given that applicants have four months from issuing proceedings in which to formally serve the same.

Being Late?

The usual time limit for making family provision claims is six months after a grant is issued, but the court has discretion to allow claims out of time (section 4, Inheritance Act 1975).

There is no statutory guidance on the factors that the court should consider when considering an application for permission to make a late claim – Re Salmon [1981] Ch 167 and Re Dennis [1981] 2 All ER 140 which include:

a) The discretion of the court is unfettered.

b) The onus is on the applicant to show special reasons for taking matter beyond six-month period.

c) The court must consider how promptly and in what circumstances the application has been made.

d) The Court must consider whether the estate has been distributed.

e) The Court can establish if negotiations commenced in the six-month period.

f) The Court must consider if the refusal to grant the applicant leave to bring proceedings to bring proceedings would leave the applicant with recourse against anyone (e.g. a negligent solicitor).

Conduct

There is no Practice Direction to the Civil Procedure Rules relating to IPFDA Claims dealing with pre-action conduct provides that, in cases not covered by any approved protocol, the court will expect the parties to act reasonably in exchanging information of relevance to the claim and generally in trying to avoid the necessity for the start of proceedings.

You can propose to follow the ACTAPS Practice Guidance for the Resolution of Probate and Trust Disputes ("the ACTAPS Code")[16], where a claim is intimated under the 1975 Act.

TIP – Keep Pushing Mediation

At this point in the early stage in the case it is a good idea to pressurise the opposing party to mediate.

It is useful to send correspondence to the other side reminding them that a refusal to mediate is likely to lead to adverse costs penalties.[17]

If resistance remains it can be quite useful to attempt to take the high moral ground and remind them to act in a reasonable and proportionate way in all dealings with each other.

---

[16] http://www.actaps.com/draft.cfm

[17] Dunnett v Railtrack 2002 EWCA Civ 302 & Halsey v Milton Keynes NHS Trust 2004 EWCA Civ 576

Proceedings

A claim under the 1975 Act is dealt with under CPR Part 57.

It is made by issuing a claim form in accordance with CPR Part 8 and doing the following:

The written evidence filed and served by the Claimant with the claim form must exhibit an official copy of the grant of probate or letters of administration and every testamentary document in respect of the grant or letters of administration.

The time within which a defendant must file and serve an acknowledgment of service and any written evidence is not more than 21 days after the service of the claim form on him or her.

Once proceedings are issued, the claim form must be served within 4 months. The Claim form should identify under which sections of the 1975 Act the claimant applies.

For cost under the CPR the general rule is that the losing party pays the winner's costs – This is subject to the Court's discretion and if the parties have acted reasonably the Court may order cost payable from the estate.

APPENDIX

APPLICATION BY SURVIVING SPOUSE UNDER THE INHERITANCE (PROVISION FOR FAMILY AND DEPENDANTS) ACT 1975

Claim No [ ]

IN THE HIGH COURT OF JUSTICE

[CHANCERY/FAMILY DIVISION]

IN THE ESTATE OF [deceased's full name] DECEASED

Details of claim

1. The Claimant applies under the Inheritance (Provision for Family and Dependants) Act 1975 as the widow of [deceased's full name] deceased who died on [date] (the 'Deceased').

2. The Defendants are the executors [and trustees] of the will dated [date of will] pursuant to a grant dated [date of grant] issued from the [registry].

3. The Deceased died domiciled in England and Wales

4. [Can insert more detail regarding the nature of the claim, provision in the will etc.]

5. The Claimant seeks the following relief:

5.1 An order that such reasonable financial provision as the Court thinks fit be made for the Claimant out of the net estate of the Deceased.

5.2 Such further or other relief.

5.3 An order that the costs of this application be paid out of the said estate.

CPR Part 8 applies to this claim.

APPENDIX: WITNESS STATEMENT IN SUPPORT OF SURVIVING SPOUSE CLAIM UNDER INHERITANCE (PROVISION FOR FAMILY AND DEPENDANTS) ACT 1975

Claim No [ ]

[[IN THE HIGH COURT OF JUSTICE]

[CHANCERY/FAMILY DIVISION]

IN THE MATTER OF THE ESTATE OF [*Deceased's full name]* DECEASED AND IN THE MATTER OF THE INHERITANCE (PROVISION FOR FAMILY AND DEPENDANTS) ACT 1975

I, [*insert name*] of [*address and occupation*], state as follows:

d) I am the above-named Claimant and I am the [widow of the above-named [*Deceased's full name*] ('the Deceased'), to whom I was married on [*date*]. There is now produced and shown to me marked [ ] a certificate of our marriage].

e) The Deceased died on [*date*] being then domiciled in England and Wales. A certificate of [his/her] death is now produced and shown to me marked [ ].

f) [By [his/her] Will dated [*date*] the Deceased bequeathed [*state provision in Will*] and appointed the [ ] and [[Defendant[s] as executor[s]] [The Deceased died intestate]. [A Grant of Probate/Grant of Letters of Administration] in relation to the estate of the Deceased was taken out on [*date*] and the Defendant[s] [is/are] the personal representative[s]. There is now produced and shown to me marked [ ] Office copy [Grant of Probate/Grant of Representation] and all testamentary documents as required by CPR, r 57.16(3)(b)

g) The net value of the Deceased's Estate for Probate purposes is £[*insert value*].

h) The disposition of the Deceased's estate [effected by [his/her] Will] [the law relating to intestacy] is not such as to make reasonable financial provision for me. The provision made [in the Will] [under intestacy] is as follows: [*Give full details*].

i) To the best of my knowledge and belief the person[s] or class[es] of person[s] interested in the estate and the nature of their interest[s] are as follows: [*Set out the legacies to the Will*].

j) My means are as follows: [*Set out all present and foreseeable financial commitments, resources and expenses*].

k) [*Set out all other facts and matters which the Claimant intends to place before the court relevant to the factors to which the court is required to have regard under s 3 of the Act. Also set out particulars of any known previous proceedings relevant to the application. Such proceedings will often be material to the question whether the application ought to be transferred from the Family Division to the Chancery Division or vice versa. Transfer of the proceedings might also be appropriate in other circumstances e.g. insufficient grounds being shown by the parties or where the application involves the taking of complicated accounts for which special facilities exist in the Chancery Division.*]

l) [*Where permission to apply out of time is sought*] I ask the Court's permission to make this application notwithstanding that the period of six months has expired from the date on which representation in regard to the estate of the Deceased was first taken out and the grounds of my request are as follows [*set out grounds – Re Salmon factors*].

m) I ask that financial provision be made for me out of the Deceased's estate by way of [*state nature of provision applied for, e.g. periodical payments, and/or lump sum and/or transfer to me of the property known as* [ ]] out the of Deceased's estate.

[*Statement of truth*]

CHAPTER THREE

EXECUTORS – CHALLENGING THE EXECUTOR

How to Deal With Difficult Executors

An executor will generally remain entitled to a grant of probate and to administer the estate in priority to anyone else (Non-Contentious Probate Rules 1987).

If an executor is being difficult, what are tools are at his or her disposal to bring the executor into order? For ease of reference what we are referring to are options which lie if the deceased died in England and Wales.

TIP

The executor is given one year to distribute the estate – As a result during that year be cautious (unless there is a risk of assets being illegally distributed) in taking action. After ten months from date of death it starts becoming a different ball game and the beneficiary/person with an interest can start by being more aggressive in challenging the executor.

Pre-grant

It is not always clear pre-grant that an executor nominated in a will is likely to be problematic, particularly where that executor is a professional. However, where trouble arises or is anticipated, the following routes can be considered.[18]

[18] An excellent article on dealing with executors is "Tackling troublesome executors" by Charlotte Black and Richard Sims, March 2009 which covers these issues in more depth – https://www.step.org/journal/step-journal-march-2009/tackling-troublesome-executors

Caveats

Often a sensible first step in stopping a grant of probate to an unsuitable executor is to enter a caveat, as it prevents a grant being made in respect of an estate (except grants ad colligenda bona or pendente lite). Indeed in some cases such as citations, a caveat is a necessary precursor.

The procedure is mostly contained in NCPR r.44. Unless warned, caveats generally remain in force for six months, unless the registrar orders otherwise but they can be extended for subsequent periods (see NCPR r.44(3)).

What are Caveats?

Caveats are a system of preventing common form grants. They are important where there are genuine concerns about the validity of a Will or the suitability of a particular person acting as executor or administrator. The caveat procedure is used to prevent a Grant of Probate or Letters of Administration being taken out in respect of a deceased's estate. The person who puts the caveat in place is called the caveator.

Why would you want to lodge a caveat?

The reasons include:

- Where the caveator wants to prevent the Grant of Probate being taken out as they believe the Will of the deceased is invalid for some reason, such as the person who made the Will did not have the mental capacity to do so, or the Will was not properly witnessed;

- Where the caveator wants to prevent a Grant of Letters of Administration being taken out on the basis that the deceased died intestate, when they believe there was a validly-executed Will in existence; or

- Where the caveator is aware of or involved in a dispute about who is entitled, or is the appropriate party, to take out the Grant of Letters of Administration.

When is it not appropriate to issue a caveat?

It is not a good idea to lodge a caveat where the caveator wishes to bring a claim under the Inheritance (Provision for Family and Dependants) Act 1975. This is because a claim under this Act can only be brought once the grant of representation has been taken out. This is a common error made. However, it can be an innexpesive way to block estates.

What is the procedure for issuing a caveat?

A caveat can be lodged at any Probate Registry; this does not need to be at the probate registry local to the deceased. The Probate Registry will need:

- The deceased's name, date of death and address;
- The name and address of the caveator;
- The request for the caveat to be signed by the caveator or their solicitor;
- A fee of £20

The caveat is then valid for six months. It can be renewed at the end of this period on payment of a further fee.

How can the caveat be removed?[19]

The caveator can remove the caveat at any time by writing to the Probate Registry. Given this a legal letter may be a good idea informing the individual that it is an abuse of proceedings to issue a Caveat inappropriately (see Parnall v Hurst [2003] WTLR 997.) 4

Any interested person may therefore issue a "warning" to the caveator. A warning is a notice to the caveator and must be in the prescribed form. A warning can only be entered at the Leeds District Probate Registry. There is no fee for issuing a warning to a caveat.

The person issuing the warning must state the nature of his interest and

[19] https://assets.publishing.service.gov.uk/government/uploads/system/uploads/attachment_data/file/905668/pa8-eng.pdf

the date of the Will (if any) in the warning and it must be served on the caveator in accordance with specific rules as to service. The warning must also require the caveator to state the nature of his interest.

Once the warning has been served on the caveator, one of the four things will happen depending on what right the caveator is alleging and what steps he chooses to take:

- The caveator may withdraw his caveat – this can be done at anytime before he enters an appearance to the warning. When a warning has been issued, then the caveator must give notice of his withdrawal to the person issuing the warning. The caveat must be withdrawn at the registry in which it was entered. No fee is payable upon the withdrawal of the caveat.

- The caveator may enter an "appearance" – an appearance should be entered in the prescribed form at the Leeds District Probate Registry within eight days of service of the warning on the caveator. If the caveator does not enter an appearance then the person issuing the warning may take steps to "warn off" the caveator. Once an appearance has been entered, the caveat remains in force until a District Judge (or, when the parties consent to the discontinuance of the caveat, a registrar) otherwise directs. There is no fee for entering an appearance.

- The caveator may issue and serve a summons for directions – this must be done within eight days of service of the warning, otherwise the caveator risks being warned off. Please note that a summons for directions may only be issued by a caveator who has no interest contrary to that of the person issuing the warning. After a summons for directions has been issued there will be a hearing before a District Judge at which he will decide to whom a grant should be made.

- A caveator may do nothing – in this case the person issuing the warning may file an affidavit in the Leeds District Probate registry after the eight-day time-limit for entering an appearance has expired. The affidavit must show that the warning was served on the caveator. The caveat is then said to be "warned off" and is no longer effective so that the person issuing the warning is then free to proceed with his application.

TIP

Caveats are an in expensive blocking tool and can actually quite effective to bring the other side to the table. Be warned that your bluff may be called and then you have to be prepared otherwise your client will face a costs award. As we see later, they must be used if you are about to issue a citation.

Renunciation

Renunciation is only an option where a nominated executor is cooperative since the executor cannot be forced to renounce.

This can only be used where an executor has not already intermeddled with the estate.

Anyone named as an executor in a will may abandon the role by signing a renunciation witnessed by a disinterested witness, ie the witness must not be mentioned in the will, and should not be a family member.

What is Intermeddling?

Intermeddling is carrying out the sort of tasks that an executor may do, such as letting a bank know of the death. If there are two executors and one is given a specific legacy and takes possession of that legacy without consent of the co-executor, this will amount to an act of administration.

This is why it is important if you do not wish to extract a grant not to take any steps in relation to the estate.

Arranging a funeral is not intermeddling.

A renunciation must be absolute, and will take effect from the time that it is signed; though it remains possible to withdraw it at any time prior to it being lodged at the probate registry.

Once it has been lodged (together with the original will, or if this is not available, a verified copy), it can only be retracted with the permission of a district judge or registrar.

Where an executor is willing and able, however, for example where he simply wants nothing to do with the administration, he may renounce, effectively abandoning his right to a grant of probate (see AEA s.5(iii)).

This allows the next entitled person (under NCPR r.20 – generally a residuary legatee), to take a grant.

The renunciation must be in writing and while this can be done any time after a testator's death. Once made, a renunciation can be retracted but only with the leave of a district judge or registrar, and only in exceptional circumstances where probate has already been granted to someone else (NCPR r.37(3)).

Citations

Where renunciation is not possible, citations are a good tactical way of trying to force a delaying executor into action, or to entitle someone else to administer the estate.

There are two main types to consider: a citation to accept or refuse a grant, and a citation to take a grant.

Citation To Accept or Refuse a Grant

- Applies where an executor has not intermeddled and cannot be persuaded to renounce.
- Is taking no steps to obtain a grant of probate, he can be cited by the person next entitled to a grant to accept or refuse probate (NCPR r.47(1)).
- If the executor fails to appear or apply for a grant, the citor is entitled to apply for a grant to himself (NCPR r.47(5)(a); 47(7)(a)).

Citation To Take A Grant

- Applies where an executor has intermeddled in the estate (so that renunciation is impossible).

- Has not taken a grant within six months of death he may be cited by any person interested in the estate to show cause why he should not be ordered to take a grant (NCPR r.47(3)).

- If the executor fails to appear or apply for a grant, the citor may apply for an order requiring the executor to take a grant (if such an order is made and breached, the executor will be liable for committal), or for a grant to himself or someone else (NCPR r.47(5)(c); 47(7)(c)).

Before any citation is issued, a caveat must be entered in respect of the estate and no court fee applies.,

TIP – Citations

As we know, probate disputes are an expensive business. Citations are a nice form of legal action as it is quite targeted, can put the executor pressure and force him or her to start dealing with the Court. Even with the most difficult executor, do not underestimate the fear which an executor can have when faced with specific Court action.

Procedure

A citation of any type may be issued by the Principal Registry or by a District Registry and must be settled by a District Judge or Registrar. (NCPR 1987 Rule 46 (1)). The application for the issue of a citation may be made in person or by post. Everyone with an interest in the document should be cited.

An affidavit should not be sworn before a citation is settled so that it can be corrected if it does not cover the required facts. Every Will or purported Will referred to in a citation must be filed.

A citation must be served personally unless otherwise directed (NCPR, Rule 46 (4)). A Certificate of Service should be endorsed.

A person who has been cited then enters an appearance at the Registry from which the citation is issued by lodging Form 5 to the NCPR.

The form sets out the name, address and interest claimed by the citor as shown on the citation. It should also give the full name, address and details of the interest of the citee himself including the date of the Will under which such interest arises.

The citee must serve a sealed copy of the appearance on the citor by delivering it at the citor's address for service or by sending it there by post or otherwise. The time for appearance is 8 days after service of the citation but it can be extended.

Passing over

Within the scope of s.116 of the Supreme Court Act 1981 the High Court may appoint someone other than a nominated executor (or any other entitled person) to administer the estate if it considers that by reason of any 'special circumstance' it would be 'necessary or expedient' to do so.

This can be over disputing co-executors, where there is a conflict of interest, and it can also be useful where the executor is thought to be of bad character, or where he is unlikely to administer the estate properly (such as in Re Biggs Estate [1966] 1 All ER 358).

The Court will take a broad view of "special circumstances" under s 116: Some other authority worth looking is re Clore decd [1982] Fam 113 (and on appeal as IRC v Stype Investments (Jersey) Ltd [1982] Ch 456) and Buchanan v Milton [1999] 2 FLR 844.

Generally the words "special circumstances" are not necessarily limited to circumstances in connection with the estate itself or its administration, but could extend to any other circumstances which the court thinks are relevant, which lead the court to think that it is necessary, or expedient, to pass over the executor.

The application is made without notice to the District Judge or registrar, with a supporting affidavit, (NCPR r.52), which must disclose all material facts to the court, otherwise the grant could be revoked (Shephard v Wheeler (2000) Times, 15 February).

Grant ad colligenda bona[20]

If the dispute looks set to continue on for some time, it is possible to consider an application for a grant ad colligenda bona defuncti.

This gives a limited grant of administration enabling the estate to be administered in the meantime for the purpose of preserving its assets.

A key aspect of a grant ad colligenda bona – and why it is attractive to the registrars and the court – is that it merely preserves, and does not allow for distribution of the estate as between competing legal parties.

It is often possible for both executors and beneficiaries to agree to this emergency measure, but it is not always an appropriate course of action, and can be an expensive and time-consuming process.

It should only be used where there is a genuine risk to the estate, and not merely to ensure a tactical advantage – see Ghafoor v Cliff [2006] 2 All ER 1079.

However, the judgment in Sifri v Clough & Willis [2007] WTLR 1453 was key of the professional executors for failing to take this precaution. Therefore, a valid method to be used by the executors.

Where a property sale needs completing or such like the procedure for a grant ad colligenda bona is simple and quick being commonly made to the registrar and can be made without notice based on an affidavit.

[20] Recently I issued one of these applications instead of making a removal of executor of application due to an executor deliberately refusing to sell the Deceased's family home. Having gone through the process I would be tempted just to go straight for removal of executor proceedings as typically even if you succeed you are left with the problem of an executor who still has to distribute the assets.

Procedure

Application for the grant must include a supporting affidavit in which the grounds for the application must be stated (NCPR r. 52). Unless the application is likely to be contentious it may be made without notice (see Ghafoor).

Post-Grant

If probate has been obtained these are the following options to bring the executor to account.

Inventory and account

My favourite application as it can achieve so much and with respect to executors who are committing fraud, it can provide access to bank accounts which fraudulent executors hate; it is also inexpensive. I have seen the most obstructive executors fold once they have faced a costs order and the threat of committal if they breach an order.

It is the quickest way to compel a lazy or uncommunicative executor to account for his activities is to apply for an order that he exhibit an inventory and account in respect of the administration (see AEA s.25(b)).

Why I Like Inventory and Account

- It is a relatively low risk application. Unlike other court actions such as removal of executor which are not certain to win despite the evidence, it is a relatively risk-free court step and clearly defined. As a consequence, there is little downside in making the application and less stress for the client to go to Court.

- It will obtain useful information whatever which in itself is useful and can provide a springboard for further steps to be taken against the executor. One of the frustrations of dealing with an executor is that there is no obligation to disclose until the end of the process when estate accounts are produced. Here the executor has to provide the information and you see a paper trail. If something dodgy is going on, you should find out. If not, you have not necessarily wasted time on other expensive legal action.

- You should get the Court date quickly. As the application is fairly short you do not have to wait a long time (e.g more than nine months to get a final court date) to go before the Judge. Resolution is relatively quick.

- It is not expensive. Unless you and your solicitor want to burn money, the Court step is not that costly and does not have a large Court fee as well. All you have to do is pay for are the legal fees and an affidavit to be sworn in front of a solicitor (say £10). Compare that to other court steps in an era when there is a deliberate strategy from the government to get money in via court fees.

- It shifts psychological power away from the executor and to the beneficiary. Whenever I have used this application with success (and it has always been successful for me), it has shifted the inter-play with the executor and put him or her on the defensive. No executor likes to disclose bank accounts and/or have costs awards made against him or her. Here the executor finds himself under pressure and subject to potential scrutiny from the Judge. If you have done something dodgy or have something to hide, you do not like this despite the targeted nature of the application.[21]

It cannot be used pre-grant.

Procedure

Prepare a Summons which is sent to the High Court together with a supporting affidavit (NCPR r. 61).

The Court will send back the sealed summons which you will send to the Respondent and you will need to produce evidence of service. The beneficiaries of an estate are entitled to request the personal representative to provide an inventory and account. This longstanding right is now contained in s. 25 of the Administration of Estates Act 1925.

---

[21] https://www.bailii.org/ew/cases/EWHC/Fam/2020/213.html

In order to get up to speed a very useful case and easy to read judgment is in the case of Ali v Taj.

This case is an excellent starting point for understanding inventory and account and restates some points at paragraph 55:

i) An order requiring the executor to provide an inventory and render an account of the administration can be enforced by means of committal proceedings (see Marshman v Brookes (1863) 32 LJPM & A 95 and Baker v Baker (1860) 2 Sw & Tr 380).

ii) Any person interested in an estate may call on the executor to exhibit and inventory and render an account of his or her administration of the estate (see Myddleton v Rushout (1797) 1 Phillim 244).

iii) An order that the executor provide an inventory of the estate and account of his or her administration of the estate can be sought at any time, even in first year following the grant of probate, during which year the executor is not bound to distribute the estate of the deceased (see Administration of Estates Act 1925 s 44) and that mere lapse of time is no bar to the discharge of the obligation (see Jickling v Bircham (1843) and Scurrah v Scurrah (1841)

iv) An executor will remain liable to provide an account of his administration of the estate even after he has been removed as an executor or his administration has expired. In In the Estate of Thomas, Deceased [1956] 1 WLR 1516 in which the court made clear that an order under s 25 of the Administration of Estates Act 1925 can be made against an executor even though he is no longer a personal representative, whether by reason of the grant having been terminated by order of the court or by a cessate grant (see also Taylor v Newton (1752) 1 Lee 15).

v) The obligation to exhibit an inventory and provide an account is not confined to the original executors, but may continue to be enforced against the executor of one of several executors, even if there is an executor of the original testator still surviving (see Pitt v Woodham (1828) 1 Hag Ecc 247 at 250).

vi) Practical or logistical difficulties in producing an account will not prevent an account being ordered. In Freeman and Fairlee (1812) 3 Mer. 44

an executor coming from India and, after 21 years, being asked to account claimed that he had left the information behind on the Indian Subcontinent. Nonetheless, the executor was ordered to produce and account within six months notwithstanding the challenges in doing so and the court recognising the likelihood that the executor would need to apply for an extension, subject to producing evidence that he was using due diligence to seek to comply with the order

Please see precedent.

TIP

One of the increasing trends of inventory and account applications is the ability to make paper Directions where the Court will make an order without arranging a hearing. This can save cost and there is still the potential to claim costs. In this scenario you can submit your statement of costs at the same time as submitting your application.

If the Respondent ignores an Inventory and Account, you can apply to obtain a Penal Notice. This is a notice endorsed on an order, providing that a defendant may be found to be guilty of contempt of court if the defendant fails to comply with the terms of the order. A penal notice is a warning to the defendant that disobedience to the order may be punishable by imprisonment, a fine, confiscation of assets or other punishment under the law (CPR 81.2)

TIP

Do not get sucked into massive costs on enforcing penal notices. If an executor ignores a penal notice the hassle and of cost of enforcing is not worth it. Just get on and start removal of executor proceedings.[22]

---

[22] If you are still minded to make a penal notice I refer you to the Civil Procedure Rules Part 81. Your client must seek permission from the Court before making a committal application. The application notice must be supported by an affidavit. You should file an Committal application together with a Part 8 Claim form with a supporting affidavit (see Civil Procedure Rules Part 81.14) The Court fee to issue the Claim form is £528.00, as it must be issued in the High Court. You will also have to pay the application fee of £255.00.

When You Do Not Use Inventory and Account – CPR PART 64

1. If the financial issues are complex. Sometimes the blunt tool of inventory and account is limited. In this case you should commence Part 64 legal proceedings [23]within the High Court as a mechanism. The downside is you face greater costs risks but on a matters of complexity Part 64 is the way to go to.

2. On matters of financial complexity you should also consider instructing a forensic accountant to give added strength to your arguments.

The Court has wide power under CPR Part 64 to direct such accounts and inquiries as necessary. Where the action is for an account it can be brought under this part and is supported by a Claim form. See precedent for wording in support.

Judicial trustee

It is also still possible for a beneficiary to apply to the court under s.1 of the Judicial Trustees Act 1896 (JTA) for the appointment by the court of a judicial trustee to administer the estate either together with the current executor, or as a replacement.

The judicial trustee is entitled to remuneration out of the estate by order of the court.

It is widely recognised that in the clear majority of cases the appointment of a judicial trustee is an unnecessarily expensive and drawn out process, and a s.50 application to replace or remove an executor will be far preferable.

Since 1985 it is no longer necessary to appoint a Judicial Trustee to continue the administration of an estate.

Thus, the Judicial Trustee Act 1896 has largely fallen into disuse. How-

[23] https://www.justice.gov.uk/courts/procedure-rules/civil/rules/part64

ever, the Official Solicitor often prefers to be appointed as a Judicial Trustee, so as to be able to make informal applications to the court for directions (see Judicial Trustee Rules 1983 r8).

Furthermore, the powers of a Judicial Trustee are wider than a personal representative, so where the estate is complicated, a Judicial Trustee may be a better choice (see Re Ridsdel [1947] Ch 597)

The application can be useful in these circumstances:

An application for a judicial trustee may be more sensible than a s.50 application is in the context of mutual wills (see Thomas and Agnes Carvel Foundation v Carvel [2007] 4 All ER 81).

Where the administration of an estate is likely to be particularly complicated for some reason. In this case, the appointment of a judicial trustee may be considered since they would have easier access to guidance and supervision from the court and can seek directions at any time. This can be more practical for all concerned but may also act as a safeguard for the beneficiaries.

Administration proceedings

Finally, the beneficiaries can make administration proceedings – Administration orders are now unusual. This is reflected in the fact that under CPR PD64 paragraph 3.1 the court will only make an administration order if it considers that the issues between the parties cannot properly be resolved in any other way. Please consider CPR PD 64.

RENUNCIATION FORM

IN THE HIGH COURT OF JUSTICE FAMILY DIVISION THE [PRINCIPAL (or) (name) DISTRICT PROBATE] REGISTRY

In the Estate of (name) deceased WHEREAS (full true name of deceased) of (full permanent private address) deceased, died on the (date) having made and duly executed (his/her) last will and testament dated (date) [with a codicil dated (date)] and in the [will (or) codicil] appointed (names of executors) as executors [and residuary legatees and devisees in trust]. Now I (name of executor) being one of the executors do declare that I have not intermeddled in the estate of the deceased, and will not hereafter intermeddle in the estate with intention to defraud creditors, and I do now renounce all my right and title to probate and execution of the will [and codicil] [and to letters of administration (with the will annexed) of the estate of the deceased]

DATED this

day of

20

SIGNED by

(name of executor)

in the presence, of

Witness Signature:

.... Witness Name:

.... Witness Address:

....

....

.... Witness Occupation:

SUMMONS FORM

IN THE HIGH COURT OF JUSTICE
PRINCIPAL REGISTRY OF THE FAMILY DIVISION
(PROBATE)

In the estate of JH (deceased)

Of xx

Who died on 31st October 20

Between JDS	Applicant
And	Respondent
Let J	attend before

The District Judge sitting in court at the Principal Registry of the Family Division, First Avenue House, 42-49 High Holborn, London WC1V 6NP at am/pm the day of 20

On the hearing of an application on the part of the Applicant

For A Request For Inventory and Account

Dated the day of 2016

(PTO)

SUMMONS FORM

IN THE HIGH COURT OF JUSTICE
PRINCIPAL REGISTRY OF THE FAMILY DIVISION
(PROBATE)

The estimated duration of the summons is minutes/hours.

Counsel will not appear on behalf of the Applicant.

This summons is taken out by:

XX LLP, (Solicitors for Applicant):

To: xxx

CHAPTER FOUR

REMOVAL OF EXECUTORS

Historically most solicitors have shied away from advising their clients to commence removal of executor proceedings.

In the right circumstances removal of executor proceedings area is a distinct possibility.

Variables

1. Has one year elapsed since the Deceased died and is the Executor justified in delaying distribution?

2. Do you have any indication of fraud from the Executor?

3. Has the Executor ignored any previous Court orders and correspondence from you?

4. Do you need the Executor to be replaced to ensure that the estate will be distributed?

5. Have you got a paper trail of correspondence illustrating that the Executor is simply not capable or interested in distributing the Estate in a correct way?

6. Are there reasons why your proposed replacement executor is not suitable?

7. Are there any weaknesses in your client's case and can they be mitigated?

What is an executor of a will?

When somebody dies, the executor named in their will ultimately has to ensure that the deceased's estate is properly wound up and their wishes in their will are carried out. There are many legal responsibilities associated with being an executor, including potentially:

- registering the death
- arranging the funeral
- valuing the estate
- paying any inheritance tax
- applying for probate
- sorting the deceased's finances
- placing a deceased estates notice
- distributing the estate
- keeping estate accounts

TIP

With cases of these kind it is really worth stepping back and establishing if the executor can be removed. It is very easy to get sucked into the emotion of the situation and form judgments either against or for the complaining party.

Generally, this type of application is used to remove a personal representative where the Grant of Probate has already been taken.

However, in Goodman v Goodman [2013] EWHC 758 (Ch), the High Court held that the court's powers under s50 of the Administration of Justice Act 1985 can be exercised before a Grant of Probate has been obtained.

The Law

Generally, the go to legislation is that of Section 50 of the Administration of Justice Act 1985 which states:

> *Power of High Court to appoint substitute for, or to remove, personal representative.*

(1) Where an application relating to the estate of a deceased person is made to the High Court under this subsection by or on behalf of a personal representative of the deceased or a beneficiary of the estate, the court may in its discretion—

(a) appoint a person (in this section called a substituted personal representative) to act as personal representative of the deceased in place of the existing personal representative or representatives of the deceased or any of them; or

(b)if there are two or more existing personal representatives of the deceased, terminate the appointment of one or more, but not all, of those persons.

(2) Where the court appoints a person to act as a substituted personal representative of a deceased person, then—

(a) if that person is appointed to act with an executor or executors the appointment shall (except for the purpose of including him in any chain of representation) constitute him executor of the deceased as from the date of the appointment; and

(b) in any other case the appointment shall constitute that person administrator of the deceased's estate as from the date of the appointment.

(3) The court may authorise a person appointed as a substituted personal representative to charge remuneration for his services as such, on such terms (whether or not involving the submission of bills of charges for taxation by the court) as the court may think fit.

(4) Where an application relating to the estate of a deceased person is made to the court under subsection (1), the court may if it thinks fit, proceed as if the application were, or included, an application for the appointment under the Judicial Trustees Act 1896 of a judicial trustee in relation to that estate.

(5) In this section "beneficiary", in relation to the estate of a deceased person, means a person who under the will of the deceased or under the law relating to intestacy is beneficially interested in the estate.

Thus, this legislation enables the High Court to do the following:

- Appoint a new executor in place of an existing executor.
- Appoint a new administrator in place of an existing administrator.
- Appoint a new administrator in place of all existing personal representatives.
- Terminate the appointment of a personal representative without replacing them, provided that this leaves at least one existing personal representative in place.

Whether a s.50 application will succeed is a matter for the discretion of the court and that the overriding considerations are broadly the proper administration of the estate and the welfare of the beneficiaries.

The statute itself provides no guidance as to the test to be applied by the court when exercising its discretion. There is a case law on the issue. Nonetheless, given the very fact specific nature of these sorts of disputes, the outcome of an application can be difficult is dependent on the lawyer to think through the evidence and plot a course of success.

It is not necessary to establish wrongdoing or fault on the part of the executor. The court will generally replace an executor where, for example, relations between him and the beneficiaries have simply broken down to such an extent that it is no longer possible to progress the administration of the estate properly.

TIP

A successful removal of executor application entails months of planning and execution unless you have cast iron evidence of fraud (have you considered instructing a forensic accountant?) and essentially once you have a paper trail of correspondence you should be good to go. Remember the key aspect of this kind of application is the need to frontload the work. Essentially your goal is to create a compelling case within the proceedings to remove the executor. If you cannot do this within the original claim form and supporting statement you are wasting your time.

In the case of Goodman v Goodman [2013] All ER 118 which involved an appeal against a decision to remove an executor under s.50 Administration of Justice Act 1985 the rationale for the appeal was that the incorrect procedure had been used by the claimants. As this was an application to remove an executor before the grant had been obtained, it was argued that the procedure under s.116 Senior Courts Act 1981 should have been used. The appeal failed.

Historically save in cases of actual wrongdoing or fraud (such as in Alkin v Raymond) the courts were reluctant to remove personal representatives. The overriding principle remains that the court will only remove an executor if it is in the interest of the proper administration of the estate and would promote the welfare of the beneficiaries, which will depend upon the peculiar facts of each case.

In the case of Riley v. Seed [2013] EWHC 4863 (Ch) friction and hostility justified removal where it had resulted in an impasse and notwithstanding that deceased had chosen executors the best way to break the impasse was to appoint an independent professional executor.

In Nwosu v. Nwosu [2018] EWHC 1529 (Ch) the court was satisfied that there was a sufficient breakdown of trust that directly impeded the administration of the estate that executors should be replaced by professional PR as 5 years since probate granted, estate consisted of properties which need to be sold but had not been.

Nevertheless, I believe by applying variables and common sense these cases are there to be won.

In a fairly recent case, the Court provided a useful reminder of the approach which will be taken by the Courts to an application for removal of personal representatives/trustees. The judge emphasised that:

The Court's power under s50 to remove personal representatives is a wide power, as is the Court's inherent jurisdiction to remove trustees (which is exercised essentially on the same principles).

Mere "falling out" between executors/trustees and beneficiaries is not sufficient and the executor/trustee should not be hostage to potentially "mischievous" allegations.

It is not necessary to find wrongdoing for removal to be ordered.

The core issues are whether there is any detriment to the beneficiaries and the efficient administration of the estate/trust by the person remaining in office. The overall interests of the beneficiaries are key.

To avoid undue delay in the administration of the estate/trust, while this is not a "summary judgment" jurisdiction, the dispute should be dealt with promptly.

Procedure

If a s.50 application is not being made in the course of existing proceedings, it should be brought in the Chancery Division of the High Court using a Part 8 Claim Form, and supported by written evidence (see CPR Part 57).

If there is more than one executor, the others must all be joined as parties, often together with the residuary beneficiaries. If a sole executor is being removed, a substitute should be sought otherwise the estate will be left unrepresented.

Applications under section 50 are governed by the Civil Procedure Rules r.57.13 and

PD57, paragraphs 12–14: and must be brought in the High Court.

All applications will be assigned to the Chancery Division.

Every personal representative of the estate shall be joined as a party.

The Court Fee is £528 within the High Court. To issue a claim for something other than money the fees are based on where you start your claim e.g. Part 8 claim and civil injunctions – fees order 1.5 and 1.8: High Court (including possession claims)

Under a part 8 Claim Form.

The application must be supported by the following:

- A certified sealed copy of the Grant of Probate or Letters of Administration.
- A witness statement setting out the reasons why the removal or substitution of the Executor is sought (referring to his disqualification)
- A witness statement of the proposed substitute's executor's capacity to act
- Draft order

WHAT SHOULD THE WITNESS STATEMENT INCLUDE?

It should exhibit the will and probate of the Deceased. This is the critical document which will make or break your case. It needs to be both comprehensive and succinct and consist of a compelling case why the Executor should be removed and the suitability of the proposed replacement executor. A draft statement is provided with Appendix 1.

TIP

Once you have your claim issued it should move along to having some form of Directions appointment before a Master. You will have two issues to consider -Preparation of the Court Bundle and a Skeleton Argument. If you do a Skeleton Argument, ensure that it is succinct and no more than two pages. Pay a lot of attention to the Trial Bundle. Do you have a set of correspondence which supports your client's case? I believe you should pay more attention to the documents within the bundle compared to a Skeleton Argument. Judges are very savvy in identifying arguments.

Section 41 of the Trustee Act 1925

If none of these provisions gives the dissatisfied beneficiary a remedy eh can consider s41 of the Trustee Act 1925, where the court may make an order appointing a new trustee or new trustees either in substitution for or in addition to any existing trustee or trustees. Trustee includes personal representative for this purpose.

It is also worth mentioning that if a personal representative has not intermeddled in the administration of the estate, he can renounce his right to probate. This is more cost effective and quicker than making an application to court, although it can only be used where the personal representative is willing to give up his right to take probate and has not intermeddled.

The judgement in Re Kershaw and there are three key points of principle emerge from Newey J's judgment:

He confirms that the general approach is the same as that in cases concerning the removal of trustees, as to which see Letterstedt v. Broers (1848) 9 App Cas 371. In short, the overriding consideration is the welfare of the beneficiaries or whether the estate is being properly administered. Newey J said that 'if anything, the court should remove a trustee more readily than an executor' (see the judgment at paragraph 10).

Newey J considered the extent to which hostility between beneficiaries and personal representatives is relevant to such an application. In Re Kershaw, the application had been made by the testatrix's son. The three executors were her two daughters and an accountant who had acted for Mrs Kershaw for many years. It was common ground between the parties that the relationship between the applicant and his two sisters had entirely broken down. Indeed, according to the personal representatives' evidence, the claim was part of a vendetta on the part of the applicant against one of his sisters. Newey J reaffirmed that mere hostility, friction or the breakdown in the relationship between the parties is not enough to warrant an executor's removal. Such hostility will only be relevant 'if it is obstructing the administration of the estate or [...] sometimes if it capable of doing so.'

In this case, the testatrix had considered carefully, even agonised over, who to appoint as her executors. The submission made on behalf of the applicant was that a testator's wishes are irrelevant because the court's overriding concern is simply the interests of the beneficiaries. Newey J disagreed. He said that a testator's choice 'is capable of being of relevance, if on no other basis than because the testator may be expected to have knowledge of the character, attitudes and relationships involved which the court will lack.'

Pre-Action disclosure Applications

An application for pre-action disclosure can be a strategic means of flushing out information from the other side to support your claim. That is, if your application pays off.

The courts are becoming increasingly reluctant to order pre–action disclosure and unsuccessful applicants are often left facing a costs bill as a result.

Under CPR 31.16, a potential party (applicant) may apply to court before proceedings have been issued to obtain disclosure of documents from another potential party (respondent). This is known as an application for pre-action disclosure (PAD).

The whole process is generally at the expense of the applicant. CPR 46.1(2) states as the general rule that the respondent is to have its costs of the application and of the disclosure exercise. Even if the application is unsuccessfully opposed, it is likely to require a finding of unreasonable conduct on the part of a respondent even to achieve the modest victory of no order as to costs of the application (SES Contracting v UK Coal [2007] EWCA Civ 791).

The court may only make an order for PAD where:

The applicant and respondent are likely to be party to proceedings. The disclosure sought falls within the scope of CPR 31.6; and an application for PAD is desirable in order to:

- dispose fairly of the anticipated proceedings.
- assist the dispute to be resolved without proceedings; or
- save costs.

By way of reminder, CPR 31.6 sets out the test for standard disclosure. This requires a party to disclose any document on which they rely and any document which adversely affects their or another party's case or supports another party's case.

If you do go down this route, be careful. From my point of view this kind of application would be a last resort.

On behalf of the Claimant
First Statement of XX
One Exhibit marked XX
Date Signed M

IN THE HIGH COURT OF JUSTICE **Claim No**

BUSINESS AND PROPERTY COURTS OF ENGLAND AND WALES

PROPERTY, TRUSTS AND PROBATE LIST (ChD)

IN THE MATTER OF THE ESTATE OF YYY

BETWEEN

MR WWW
Claimant

And

MS Z Z
Defendant

STATEMENT OF MR WWW

I WWW, of 2PX do say as follows:

1. I am the Claimant and the residuary beneficiary of the estate of W "The Deceased" who died while resident in England and Wales on 27th November 2018.

2. This witness statement is made in support of an application under Section 50 of Administration of Justice Act 1985 for amongst other things the removal of the executor, Ms ZZ as the sole executor of the Deceased and her replacement by my wife, R who I believe is best

placed to be an executor due to problems with my health(I have a terminal medical condition) and the fact that my wife is fully aware of my personal affairs and she is capable of administering the estate.

3. I have provided at pages of 7 to 11 inclusive of the numbered bundles of pages exhibited to this statement and marked WWW one copy of the Will and grant of Probate issued on 29th July 2019 out of N District Probate Registry.

4. The reasons for the application are as follows.

5. The Deceased made a will dated 20th June 20 appointing the Defendant and me as a residuary beneficiary, with the Defendant acting as sole executor and Trustee. After the Deceased died, the Defendant instructed the law firm, L Solicitors who had prepared the Deceased's will and afterwards helped the Defendant obtain probate on 29th May which stated the probate had a gross value of £

6. Since obtaining probate the Defendant has done little else to progress the estate including failing to try to sell of the house of the Deceased which she lives in, which is believed to be the main asset of the Deceased. Moreover, I have not received any money of my inheritance nor any form of update from the Defendant. I have only found what has been going on by contacting L Solicitors who due to the inaction of the Defendant have been limited in what they can say and do. I only found out the date that probate has been obtained and value of the estate by doing an online search myself.

7. Given this impasse and the fact that it was more than one year since the Deceased died, on 13th March 20 I instructed my solicitors, FF to write to the Defendant, copying BL Solicitors in and setting my concerns over the fact that I had not received any inheritance and any news about the progress of the estate. Also, my instructing solicitors, FF warned that if we did not receive an interim estate account within 14 days, my firm would make an application for inventory and account.

8. As a result of the lack of response, I have made an application for an inventory and account of the Deceased's estate within the N Probate Registry. In addition, my solicitors wrote on 3r to Ms Z informing her of this but heard nothing. I am still waiting to hear further from this Court to hear more about the status of my application.

9. On 21st May 20 my solicitors again wrote to the Defendant sending a Letter Before Action warning Ms Z that I was going to make an application for her removal as executor and setting out these reasons for doing so. The reasons included:

    i) Her failure to distribute the estate within 12 months of the Deceased passing away.
    ii) The fact she remained in the sole property of the Deceased, GGG with no apparent intention of moving out.
    iii) She had ignored our request for inventory and account and not provided the financial information as requested.
    iv) The fact I had concerns the gross value of the estate may be undervalued.

As a result of the above, I believe it is the interests of justice that the Defendant should be removed as executor and I request the Court grant me the relief sought in the form of the attached order.

I believe the facts stated are true

Signed ....

Dated ....

CHAPTER FIVE

TRUSTS

What is a Trust?

A trust is a way where one person (the 'settlor') may give away the enjoyment of assets to one or more individuals (the 'beneficiaries') while control and decisions on the administration and investment of those assets lies with others (the 'trustees').

Why have a Trust?

According to STEP there are a number of benefits in having a trust including:

- You can avoid probate – Where assets are transferred to a trust they are outside the estate of what is termed the settlor. This avoids the need to deal with those assets in the event of the settlor's death.

- Trusts for children/grandchildren – Parents or grandparents often create flexible trusts for the benefit of children or grandchildren who may be too young or financially unsophisticated to benefit from an outright gift. Trusts provide a mechanism for the long-term retention and control of assets.

- Trusts for those who are disabled – A trust can be used to hold and administer assets for those who are unable to hold assets themselves, e.g. minors or the mentally disabled.

- Trusts to protect assets – Trusts can be used in certain limited circumstances to protect the settlor's assets from creditors, disinherited heirs, claims by the ex-spouses or former civil partners of children or grandchildren and the risks associated with political instability. Often it is sensible to use trusts based in a different country from the settlor for this purpose.

- A settlor may wish to encourage his or her children to become involved in the family company but is possibly unsure of the relative extent to which one child or another should benefit. If he or she transfers the shares to a trust, the settlor can remain in control of the company (subject to tax considerations) by acting as one of the trustees and can thereby continue to exercise voting control over the shares gifted into trust.

What are some of the key definitions which help in understanding trusts?

Trusts involve:

- the 'settlor' – the person who puts assets into a trust
- the 'trustee' – the person who manages the trust
- the 'beneficiary' – the person who benefits from the trust

What does the settlor do?

The settlor decides how the assets in a trust should be used – this is usually set out in a document called the 'trust deed'. The settlor is the person who provides the assets of the trust. Unless he is a beneficiary or reserves powers to himself in the trust deed he has no rights over the trust assets once they are transferred to the trustees.

Sometimes the settlor can also benefit from the assets in a trust – this is called a 'settlor-interested' trust and has special tax rules. Find out more by reading the information on different types of trust.

What do trustees do?

The trustees are the legal owners of the assets held in a trust. The trustees hold the legal title to the assets upon trust for the beneficiaries. Their duty is to administer the assets in the trust and, eventually, to distribute them in accordance with the terms of the trust deed. Their role is to:

- deal with the assets according to the settlor's wishes, as set out in the trust deed or their will
- manage the trust on a day-to-day basis and pay any tax due
- decide how to invest or use the trust's assets

If the trustees change, the trust can continue, but there always should be at least one trustee.

Beneficiaries

There might be more than one beneficiary, like a whole family or defined group of people. They may benefit from:

- the income of a trust only, for example from renting out a house held in a trust
- the capital only, for example getting shares held in a trust when they reach a certain age
- both the income and capital of the trust

What are the main types of trust?

The main types of trust are:

- bare trusts
- interest in possession trusts
- discretionary trusts
- accumulation trusts

- mixed trusts
- settlor-interested trusts
- non-resident trusts

Bare trusts

Assets in a bare trust are held in the name of a trustee. However, the beneficiary has the right to all of the capital and income of the trust at any time if they're 18 or over (in England and Wales), or 16 or over (in Scotland). This means the assets set aside by the settlor will always go directly to the intended beneficiary.

Bare trusts are often used to pass assets to young people – the trustees look after them until the beneficiary is old enough.

Example:

You leave your sister some money in your will. The money is held in trust.

Your sister is entitled to the money and any income (for example interest) it earns. She can also take possession of any of the money at any time.

Interest in possession trusts

These are trusts where the trustee must pass on all trust income to the beneficiary as it arises (less any expenses).

Example:

You create a trust for all the shares you owned.

The terms of the trust say that when you die, the income from those shares go to your wife for the rest of her life. When she dies, the shares will pass to your children.

Your wife is the income beneficiary and has an 'interest in possession' in the trust. She does not have a right to the shares themselves.

Discretionary trusts

These are where the trustees can make certain decisions about how to use the trust income, and sometimes the capital.

Depending on the trust deed, trustees can decide:

- what gets paid out (income or capital)
- which beneficiary to make payments to
- how often payments are made
- any conditions to impose on the beneficiaries

Discretionary trusts are sometimes set up to put assets aside for:

- a future need, like a grandchild who may need more financial help than other beneficiaries at some point in their life
- beneficiaries who aren't capable or responsible enough to deal with money themselves

Accumulation trusts

This is where the trustees can accumulate income within the trust and add it to the trust's capital. They may also be able to pay income out, as with discretionary trusts.

Mixed trusts

These are a combination of more than one type of trust. The different parts of the trust are treated according to the tax rules that apply to each part.

Settlor-interested trusts

These are where the settlor or their spouse or civil partner benefits from the trust. The trust could be:

- an interest in possession trust
- an accumulation trusts
- a discretionary trust

Example:

You can no longer work due to illness. You set up a discretionary trust to make sure you have money in the future.

You're the settlor – you may also benefit from the trust because the trustees can make payments to you.

Non-resident trusts

This is a trust where the trustees aren't resident in the UK for tax purposes. The tax rules for non-resident trusts are very complicated.

What Are the legal obligations of trustees?

1. To exercise reasonable care and skill

Section 1 of the Trustee Act 2000 provides a general duty of care that is applicable to both trustees and PRs. The duty applies to specific situations defined in the Act, such as investing trust funds or acquiring land. Where the duty applies, a trustee must use such care and skill as is reasonable in the circumstances.

For trustees with professional knowledge or trustees acting in the course of business, i.e. professional trustees, a higher standard of care will be expected, in line with their additional knowledge.

In addition, there is a common law duty of care to act in the best interests of the beneficiaries even if this conflicts with the trustee's personal beliefs.

The standard of care applicable is that expected of a prudent businessman managing affairs for someone he felt morally bound to provide for and depends on the individual's skills and expertise.

The Will or trust instrument may exclude the duty of care and may exclude trustees' liability for breach of duty.

2. To act in the best interests of the beneficiaries as a whole

- Trustees should not favour one beneficiary over the others. This means that they should maintain a balance between the beneficiaries. For example, trustees of a life interest trust should not prefer the interests of the remainderman over those of the life tenant or vice versa.[24]

- Where the testator or settlor had a personal connection to the life tenant but not to the remainderman, the PRs or trustees can prefer the interests of the beneficiary known to the testator of settler to a certain extent. This does not, however, allow them to exclude the interests of the remainderman entirely (Nestlé v. National Westminster Bank plc [1993] 1 WLR 1260). Duties and Responsibilities of Trustees and Personal Representatives.

- Not to be remunerated for services provided unless authorised.

- It is common now for a Will or trust instrument to provide for PRs and trustees, particularly professionals, to be paid.

- A professional PR or trustee can be paid if all his fellow PRs or trustees agree in writing, even if the Will or trust instrument does not specify this (s.29(2) Trustee Act 2000). This provision does not apply to sole PRs or trustees or to charity trustees. A sole PR

[24] Lloyds Bank plc v Duker [1987] 1 WLR 1324 where it was held that shares in a private company should not be divided between the beneficiaries as this would give one beneficiary control of the company and therefore favour him beyond what the testator had intended.

or trustee of a non-charitable trust will therefore need to appoint a co-trustee to receive remuneration if this is not expressly authorised by the Will or Trust Instrument.

- Not to use trust property for private advantage A trustee may not sell trust property to himself nor make a secret profit from the trust as there is a conflict between the trustee's fiduciary duty and his personal interest.[25]

3. To obey the terms of the trust

In the case of a Will trust, the terms will normally be found in the Will.

If trustees act outside the terms they will be in breach of trust.[26]

4. To invest trust funds properly

Trustees have a duty to preserve the trust fund which implies a duty to invest any money not required for current use. This includes a duty to convert any improper funds into sensible assets, e.g. to convert investments in a life interest trust which only produce capital to income producing investments.

Trustees should obtain the best rate of return available.

The Trustee Act 2000 provides trustees with a general power of investment to invest as if they were absolutely entitled to the assets of the trust.

Before exercising their powers of investment, trustees must obtain and consider proper advice on the suitability of the proposed investment unless they reasonably conclude that in all the circumstances it is unnecessary or inappropriate to do so.

Trustees must also review their investments from time to time to consider

---

[25] Re Thompson's Settlement [1986] Ch 99 where it was held that a transaction involving two trustees could not stand once it had been called into question by a beneficiary.

[26] Target Holdings Ltd v Redferns [1996] AC 421 at 434 where it was held that a solicitor who was holding a lender's money on trust for completion of a purchase but paid the money out 10 days beforehand was in breach of trust.

whether they should be varied considering the standard investment criteria.

What are key problem areas/focuses of litigation?

Accounts?

Executors (who are not necessarily trustees) do not have a duty to inform beneficiaries of their interests, the distinction being that a Will is a public document. However, in the case of a Will establishing a trust, assuming the executors and trustees are the same people, once the administration of the estate is complete the executors will become trustees and will then have a duty to inform beneficiaries of their interests.

A trustee must keep clear and accurate accounts (Springett v Dashwood (1860) 2 Giff 521).

A beneficiary theoretically has the right to see the accounts (Armitage v Nurse [1998] Ch 241).

A beneficiary does not have the right to be given other information about the trust but may apply to the Court for an Order requiring the trustees to produce this information. He or she is likely to be granted access to the information if his or her request is reasonable, as in Schmidt v. Rosewood Trust [2003] UKPC 26).

Appropriate delegation?

Not to delegate duties unless authorised.

The Trustee Act 2000 (s.11) allows trustees to appoint agents to exercise any of their delegable functions. The functions that trustees are not allowed to delegate include: any function relating to whether or in what way any assets of the trust should be distributed.

For both estate and trust administration, there exists a clear duty to ascertain the assets and liabilities, and to administer these according to the terms of the will or trust deed, and the law. Appropriate records should therefore be maintained which will enable them to successfully do so.

What documents should be retained?

For an estate administration, the main documents to retain must include the Will and Codicils (where applicable); the original sealed Grant of Representation (plus copies); any Instruments of Variation; original death certificates; and copy birth or marriage certificates for beneficiaries whose entitlements are determined by age, or those who have married since execution of the Will.

The same approach to record-keeping applies to the administration of trusts. A trust may arise out of an estate administration, and therefore the retention of the above documents will also be essential in ensuring that an ongoing trust is administered appropriately from the outset.

Trustees must be familiar with the terms of the trust (Hallows v Lloyd (1888)), and must be prepared to produce on request any documents or information about the trust, including the trust deed as in Manning v Commissioner of Taxation (1928)

What are the duties to maintain records?

With respect to documents trustees should maintain

- trustees minutes;
- details of appointments out;
- instruments;
- adding assets to the trust;
- completion statements;
- deeds retiring or appointing new trustees;
- beneficiaries' names and addresses;

- copy birth or marriage certificates where appropriate; and any documents sent to, or received from HMRC are important;

- copies of any legal advice or opinions, to demonstrate that they have taken advice where appropriate, and to determine the reasoning behind their decisions.

How much delegation can trustees do?

Under the Trustee Act 2000 (ss11-15) a trustee may delegate authority to a stockbroker, but must be aware of any activity.[27]

The Trustee Act 2000's duty of care allows the delegation of certain duties but a trustee must still keep securities under review to avoid becoming personally liable for the acts of an agent – any records should therefore be as available, and as up to date, as is practicable.

Both PRs and trustees must be aware of what is happening at any stage in the administration, to varying degrees (dependent upon the terms and complexity of the trust and the assets held).

As both PRs and trustees' have a duty to distribute to the correct beneficiaries and in the correct proportions, this surely cannot be achieved without suitably detailed accounts in place.

Trust accounts should record all transactions during the accounting period.

As with PRs, a trustee's duty of care is also set out by statute (s1 Trustee Act 2000 expanded upon in Schedule 1).

Case law lays down trustees' duty of care, such as in Speight v Gaunt (1883) where it was established that a trustee should exercise the same care as an ordinary, prudent businessperson would exercise in conducting

[27] Nestle v National Westminster Bank (1993) found that trustees must review investments (at least annually if not more often), and considered the level to which trustees should consider a beneficiary's tax position.

that business as if it were their own.

As with business accounts, trust accounts must maintain a clear and an accurate accounting of actions taken by recording each step taken, through maintaining accounts backed up by the appropriate paperwork.

Providing records?

Some documents will already form part of the public record and may therefore be reviewed by anyone requesting a copy, regardless of a PR or a Trustees' views, such as death certificates and Wills or codicils admitted to probate.

In an estate, residuary beneficiaries and legatees may also see the accounts.

If an estate is insolvent, disappointed beneficiaries and creditors whose liabilities have been reduced or depleted may also see the accounts (s34 Administration of Estates Act 1925), as can parents or guardians of minor beneficiaries.

Beneficiaries with a defined interest in a trust (such as capital or income beneficiaries) are entitled to see the accounts, as well as the parents of minors (as before) and the Court, on request.

In Armitage v Nurse (1998) it was held that there was a core of obligations owed by a trustee to beneficiaries which were fundamental to the concept of a life interest trust, one such obligation being to account for the administration of a trust.

A beneficiary with a life interest has a right to know of the trust's existence, and his or her interest. (Brittlebank v Goodwin (1868).

Disclosure of documents in discretionary trusts, however, can provide far more uncertainty for trustees.

In the case of Cowin, Cowin v Gravett (1886) considered that beneficial ownership gives a beneficiary some prima facie right to inspect documents.

The case of Re Londonderry's Settlement (1964) lays down what trust documents should be made available to a beneficiary, mentioning trust deeds, deeds of appointment and accounts. However, documents not to be disclosed included trustees' meeting agendas, correspondence between trustees; trustees' minutes; and documents showing the reasoning behind trustees.'

How Do You Go About Attacking the Conduct of an Errant Trustee?

The Trust Instrument

First focus on the trust instrument. This is a key document, which trustees should disclose to beneficiaries if requested. The same applies to supplemental documents such as:

- Deeds of appointment and retirement of trustees.
- Instruments adding assets to the trust.
- Instruments varying the trust.

The trustees may wish to redact information that does not relate to the beneficiary making the request (for example, by obscuring the names of other beneficiaries in a deed). If a beneficiary requests redacted information, the trustees ought to inquire why (there might be a valid reason, so they should not refuse outright).

The trust instrument is the document which creates or sets out the terms of the trust. It can be something as straightforward as a will which leaves assets to minor children, a settlement deed or declaration of trust comprising many pages.

Whatever it is, there is a pretty good chance that it will set out, or refer to / amend legislation which sets out, the trustees' powers and duties.

It may also set out the person or persons who may or may not appoint, remove, or substitute trustees of the trust and how they can do that. e.g many trusts provide for no fewer than two trustees with power to appoint and remove trustees and some trusts extend that power to beneficiaries acting unanimously or, particularly in the case of offshore trusts, to protectors.

Focus on the legislation

Trustees can also be removed without the court's intervention by fellow trustees if one or more of many conditions is met. These conditions are set out in s.36 Trustee Act 1925 which provides:

> "*(1) Where a trustee, either original or substituted, and whether appointed by a court or otherwise, is dead or remains out of the United Kingdom for more than twelve months, or desires to be discharged from all or any of the trusts or powers reposed in or conferred on him, or refuses or is unfit to act therein, or is incapable of acting therein, or is an infant, then, subject to the restrictions imposed by this Act on the number of trustees, —*
>
> *(a) the person or persons nominated for the purpose of appointing new trustees by the instrument, if any, creating the trust; or*
>
> *(b) if there is no such persons, or no such person able and willing to act, then the surviving or continuing trustees or trustee for the time being, or the personal representatives of the last surviving or continuing trustee; may, by writing, appoint one or more other persons (whether or not being the persons exercising the power) to be a trustee or trustees in the place of the trustee so deceased, remaining out of the United Kingdom, desiring to be discharged, refusing, or being unfit or being incapable, or being an infant, as aforesaid.*"

Also consider s.36 (9) Trustee Act 1925 which lays down that where a trustee who lacks capacity is also a beneficiary of the trust then it is necessary to make an application for that person's removal to the Court of Protection; the court which deals with matters of physical and mental welfare.

How to Prove That the Trustee Is Unfit?

This can be very subjective and will be disputed. Being 'unfit' depends on the circumstances of the case.

Generally, a person who has been made bankrupt or convicted of a fraudulent offence will most likely be deemed to be unfit to act as will a trustee guilty of a significant breach of trust or of acting in a way which causes a conflict as between their personal position and their duty to the beneficiaries, known as their 'fiduciary duty'.

Even if a trustee is removed under s.36 Trustee Act 1925, it is entirely possible that they could challenge such a decision by way of court action.

Further, as is clear from s.36 Trustee Act 1925, this remedy is not automatically available to beneficiaries unless they are also trustees or they have power to remove trustees under the trust instrument.

Court intervention

If none of the above remedies are available then, then focus on the court to remove a trustee.

What are the Legal Ways to Remove a Trustee?

The court can remove a trustee either by statutory power (under s.41 Trustee Act 1925) or under its inherent authority.

s.41(1) Trustee Act 1925 provides:

> "*The court may, whenever it is expedient to appoint a new trustee or new trustees, and it is found inexpedient difficult or impracticable so to do without the assistance of the court, make an order appointing a new trustee or new trustees either in substitution for or in addition to any existing trustee or trustees, or although there is no existing trustee.*
>
> *In particular and without prejudice to the generality of the foregoing provision, the court may make an order appointing a new trustee in substitution for a trustee who lacks capacity to exercise his functions as trustee, or is a bankrupt, or is a corporation which is in liquidation or has been dissolved.*"

As such, and assuming there is no other method open to a party to remove a trustee, the court may do so under s.41 Trustee Act 1925 where a trustee lacks capacity, is bankrupt or, if a corporation, in liquidation or has been dissolved.

If seeking to remove a trustee under s.41 Trustee Act 1925, you should ensure you have a replacement or substitute trustee available and that trustee should file at court what is known as a 'consent to act'; a witness statement confirming the proposed replacement trustee's agreement to act as a trustee.

This should be filed along with a 'fitness to act'; a statement by somebody who knows the trustee and can vouch for their standing and suitability to act as a trustee.[28]

Each case will be considered on its own facts.

A key case is Letterstedt v Broers (1884) 9 App Cas 371 in which Lord Blackburn, sitting in the South African court, said

> "*the acts or omissions must be such as to endanger the trust property or to shew a want of honesty, or a want of proper capacity to execute the duties, or a want of reasonable fidelity*";
>
> "*It must always be borne in mind that trustees exist for the benefit of those to whom the creator of the trust estate has given the trust estate*"; and
>
> "*friction or hostility between trustees and the immediate possessor of the trust estate is not of itself a reason for the removal of the trustees. But where the hostility is grounded on the mode in which the trust has been administered.,.it is certainly not to be disregarded.*"

Breaking the Trust

Another method which can achieve the same aims is to break the trust.

The principle is laid down in the case of Saunders v Vaultier (1841) Cr & Ph 240, which should be familiar to most trust and estate lawyers, and confirms that beneficiaries who are over 18, have capacity and, together, are absolutely entitled to the trust property i.e. unanimous, can 'break

[28] cf Letterstedt v Broers (1884) 9 App Cas 371

the trust'.

This mirrors the language of s.19 Trusts of Land and Appointment of Trustees Act 1996.

In short, this means that the beneficiaries can bring the trust to an end and take their respective shares or, in the case of a life interest or discretionary trust, agree amongst themselves how much each should receive.

How should trustees deal with requests for information by beneficiaries?

If a beneficiary requests information about the trust, the trustees should bear in mind that the beneficiary has no entitlement as of right. The trustees have discretion and should conduct a balancing exercise, considering all the relevant circumstances at the time. They should consider what is in the best interests of the beneficiaries as a whole. They should also consider what the purpose of the request is. Whether or not they decide to exercise their discretion to disclose may depend on the type of document requested.

Trust Accounts

Trustees have a duty to keep clear trust accounts and to be constantly ready with those accounts. "Being ready" with the accounts is important and trustees who are slow in producing accounts are likely to be penalised in costs (West v Lazard Brothers [No 1] [1987-88] JLR 414). Therefore, if a beneficiary requests a copy of the trust accounts, the trustees should provide a copy. If they do not, the beneficiary can seek the accounts via the court, and the court usually orders the trustees to pay personally (not from the trust fund) the costs of obtaining the order.

If a beneficiary seeks disclosure of trust accounts apparently in order to attack the trust or trust property (such as a challenge to the validity of the trust which would be against the interests of the beneficiaries as a whole) the trustees ought to be cautious. If the trustees are unsure of the reason for the request, they should clarify that with the beneficiary before making a decision. However, there is a strong presumption in favour of disclosure. The trustees' concerns can usually be relieved by obtaining a confidentiality undertaking from the beneficiary that restricts the use of the accounts in other proceedings.

Henchley v Thompson [2017] EWHC 225 (Ch), where the court ordered the defendant to provide an account to the beneficiaries of his dealings with a trust of which he had been a trustee (or de facto trustee) up to the early 1990s, is reminder that the duty to account to beneficiaries is a core duty and can still be relevant after many years.

In the case of Lewis v Tamplin ([2018] EWHC 777 Ch) the London High Court was asked to exercise its jurisdiction to supervise trustees in the performance of their obligations by requiring trustees to give disclosure of documents requested by certain beneficiaries. The case also serves as a reminder of the rules regarding privilege between trustees and beneficiaries. We consider this case further below.

In some circumstances, it may be appropriate for trustees to limit the information provided to a beneficiary. For example, where there are sub-funds, it may be appropriate to ensure that the beneficiary sees only the information relating to the sub-fund in which he has an interest.

The Judge emphasised that beneficiaries have a right to hold trustees to account and to ask them for information regarding the performance of their obligations under the trust. If the trustees refuse to divulge such information then the beneficiaries can ask the Court to order the disclosure of documents containing the information, using the Court's inherent jurisdiction to supervise trustees in performance of their obligations. However, if a request is made for information which is not in documentary form then it is not certain that an order for disclosure will be made. First, the beneficiaries would have to meet the cost of turning the information into a documentary form. Secondly, beneficiaries are not entitled to receive information regarding "why" a trustee made certain decisions.

Trustees need to carefully consider whether to disclose information, and remember that the Court can order the disclosure of information using its inherent jurisdiction.

Trustees should also note that beneficiaries do not have to prove that there is a "real suspicion", but rather the Court will decide whether it is proper for them to interfere.

Additionally trustees are reminded that the Court may not view it positively if disclosures are only made begrudgingly and upon the imminent threat of legal action.

From the perspective of beneficiaries, they must ensure that document requests are framed properly and not overly wide or seeking information (as opposed to documents).

Proceedings

TIP

Like much of High Court litigation you have to do a lot of front-loading with cases if you issue proceedings namely you do a Claim form together with a statement. Hopefully within the statement you have a paper trail of correspondence showing the evasivness of the Trustee(s).

Proceedings under s. 41 of the Trustee Act 1925 should normally be commenced by a Part 8 claim form [29] (on the basis that there is no substantial dispute of fact).

Under the Part 8 procedure written evidence is served with the Claim Form. The defendants have 14 days within which to acknowledge service and file their evidence. However, this may be extended by written agreement by a further 14 days.

All the trustees should be parties. The beneficiaries should also be joined, unless perhaps they have consented to the application. The settlor (if alive) and any person nominated to appoint new trustees should also be joined.

If there is a substantial dispute of fact, the proceedings should be brought pursuant to the inherent jurisdiction of the court by way of a Part 7 claim

[29] https://www.justice.gov.uk/courts/procedure-rules/civil/rules/part64

form. However, those proceedings may include a claim for the appointment of new trustees pursuant to s. 41 of the Trustee Act 1925. The proceedings should be brought in the Chancery Division of the High Court (unless the value of the trust fund does not exceed £30,000, in which case it can be brought in the County Court).

When considering an application under section 41 of the Trustee Act 1925 the court used to object to the appointment of a beneficiary unless this could not be avoided (Re Harrop's Trust (1882) 24 Ch.D. 717 and Re Paines Trusts (1885) 33 WR 564) but, these days, if no independent trustee is available the court often appoints beneficiaries. However, the court is unlikely to appoint beneficiaries that are unwilling to act or where it is going to be difficult for a particular beneficiary to manage inherent conflicts of interest.

The application may be made by a beneficiary or a trustee (s. 58 of the Trustee Act 1925). The jurisdiction does not apply to personal representatives (s. 41(4)). However, there is a separate jurisdiction relating to the appointment and removal of personal representatives under section 50 of the Administration of Justice Act 1985 which we cover in a separate chapter.

The court has power to appoint a new trustee or trustees in substitution for any existing trustee or trustees provided that (a) it is expedient to make the appointment and (b) it is inexpedient, difficult or impracticable to do so without the assistance of the court. The court, therefore, has a statutory power to remove a trustee, but only in conjunction with the appointment of a new trustee or trustees.

CHAPTER SIX

LASTING POWERS OF ATTORNEY

What is a Lasting Power of Attorney?

A Lasting Power of Attorney (LPA) is useful tool when people become incapable of running their own financial affairs. An LPA allows someone, of the donor's choice, to step in and take control of the donor's finances.

Because of the great power the LPA gives them, attorneys are often trusted friends or family of the donor. However, where attorneys abuse this power, measures must be taken to protect the donor. This is particularly important when the donor cannot protect themselves or even complain about the way their attorney is acting.

LPAs represent a clear opportunity for people to conduct financial abuse.[30]

Adults aged 18 or over with the capacity to make decisions can make provision for the event that sometime in the future they may lack capacity to make certain decisions.

This can be done by giving another person Lasting Power of Attorney (LPA) – the authority to act on their behalf or by making advance decisions to refuse medical treatment.

People given formal powers under LPA to make decisions on behalf of adults who lack capacity are bound by the Mental Capacity Act and its Code of Practice. They have a statutory responsibility to act within the limits of the powers given to them always to act in the person's best interests

---

30 https://www.lawgazette.co.uk/law/i-would-never-sign-a-power-of-attorney-retired-judge/5062465.article

Adults who lack capacity and do not have such formal arrangements and require significant decisions to be made may be subject to a best interest meeting or the issue may need to be taken to the Court of Protection. The court may appoint a deputy to act as decision maker or make a declaration about what is in the person's best interests.

Lasting Powers of Attorney

There are two types of LPA: personal welfare and property and affairs.

LPAs are legal documents and are only valid if completed on the statutory form

LPAs must be signed by the donor

LPAs should normally name people who should be informed when it is to be registered

LPAs must contain a certificate completed by an independent third party

LPAs must name the person (or persons) who is to act as attorney

LPAs must be registered with Office of Public Guardian (OPG) before they can be used

If registered some time ago and not used, the attorney should inform the OPG when they start to act under it

LPAs may have restrictions or conditions. There are some decisions that can never be delegated to an attorney

Attorneys should never be a professional/paid carer who is or is likely to be involved in the adults' care or treatment – the only possible exception being that they are a close relative

Attorneys can only make decisions prescribed in LPA, and must carry out the donor's instructions, i.e. they cannot assume decision-making for any other matters

They may be consulted, if appropriate, over other matters unless there are explicit instructions not to

Property and affairs attorneys should keep accounts. An LPA regarding finance would be immediately effective unless the person specified at the time that this should not occur until they have lost capacity to make decisions in this area.

Enduring Power of Attorney

An enduring power of attorney (EPA) is a document that appoints someone ('an attorney') to help manage your property, money and financial affairs.

Your attorney will be able to help you make decisions or make decisions on your behalf if, for example, you have an accident or become ill and cannot make a certain decision at the time it needs to be made (you 'lack mental capacity').

The EPA was replaced with the property and financial affairs lasting power of attorney (LPA) in October 2007. You can set up a new LPA.

If you made an EPA that was signed and witnessed before October 2007 you can either:

- continue to use it
- cancel it and set up a property and financial affairs LPA
- You can also make a health and welfare LPA.
- Use an enduring power of attorney
- While you still have mental capacity, you can allow your attorney to use an EPA to help manage your finances.
- You or your attorney will need to show signed copies of your EPA to banks and financial providers so your attorney can manage your accounts.

- You cannot change an existing EPA. Cancel it and set up an LPA instead.

Court of Protection

What does the Court of Protection do?

The Court of Protection is the specialist court for all issues relating to people who lack capacity to make specific decisions. The Court can make decisions and appoint deputies to make decisions about someone's property and financial affairs or their healthcare and personal welfare.

Under the Mental Capacity Act, the Court has the power to:

- make decisions about the personal welfare or property and financial affairs of people who lack the capacity to make such decisions themselves.

- make declarations about a person's capacity to make a decision, if the matter of whether they can make a decision cannot be resolved informally.

- make decisions in relation to serious medical treatment cases, which relate to providing, withdrawing or withholding treatment to a person who lacks capacity.

- appoint a Deputy to make ongoing decisions on behalf of a person who lacks capacity, in relation to either the person's personal welfare or property and financial affairs; and

- make decisions about a Lasting Power of Attorney or Enduring Power of Attorney, including whether the power is valid, objections to registration, the scope of Attorney powers and the removal of Attorney powers.

The Office of the Public Guardian

The Public Guardian is responsible under the Mental Capacity Act for:

- supervising deputies appointed by the Court of Protection.
- keeping registers of deputies, Lasting Powers of Attorney, and Enduring Powers of Attorney; and
- investigating any complaints about attorneys or deputies.

The Court of Protection has the power to:

- decide whether a person has capacity to decide for themselves
- make declarations, decisions or orders affecting people who lack capacity to make decisions
- appoint deputies to make decisions for people who lack capacity
- decide the validity of LPAs and remove deputies or attorneys who fail to carry out their duties appropriately

Who can make applications to the court?

Anyone can make an application if they feel they have just cause. Usually people making applications will be:

- vulnerable adults who feel they have been unfairly determined as lacking capacity to decide
- family members who disagree amongst themselves or with an agency about what's in the best interests of the person lacking capacity
- family or friends who wish to seek authority to manage the affairs of a person who is lacking capacity to make decisions about their own affairs

- NHS Trusts which need to make a major decision about serious medical treatment for a person who lacks capacity

- local authorities which have concerns about major decisions affecting the person's welfare

The court can appoint deputies who are adults (8+ years who manage either the person lacking capacity's property and affairs or welfare decisions. A deputy could be a family member or a professional (though not a paid carer directly involved in the care or treatment of the person)

The scope and limits of a deputy's authority will be clearly determined in the order of appointment

Deputies must act in accordance with all the act's statutory principles, especially best interests and have regard to the code of practice.

However, it may be necessary to apply to court for an order, if the enduring power of attorney or a lasting power of attorney does not permit the attorney to make the decision in question (for example there may be restrictions or conditions in the power); or if the attorney is prevented from doing something by the Act or any other law (for example the Act does not allow the attorney to make a will on behalf of someone else). In such circumstances, the attorney will need to apply to court.

What Are the Fees?

You must pay a fee to apply to be a deputy. You must also pay a supervision fee every year after you've been appointed.

When you apply

You must pay a £400 application fee. Send this with your application form.

You need to pay the application fee twice if you're applying to become both types of deputy.

You'll also need to pay £500 if the court decides your case needs a hearing. The court will tell you when you need to pay this.

Make all cheques payable to 'HM Courts and Tribunals Service'.

After you've been appointed

You must pay an annual supervision fee depending on what level of supervision your deputyship needs. You'll pay:

£320 for general supervision

£35 for minimal supervision (if you're a property and affairs deputy managing less than £21,000)

Your annual supervision fee is due on 31 March for the previous year.

You'll also need to pay a £100 assessment fee if you're a new deputy.

The Office of the Public Guardian will tell you how and when to pay your assessment and supervision fees.

You may be able to claim a refund of your fees in certain situations.

Before the Court of Protection releases a deputyship order, it requires the deputy to put in place a security bond. The level of the bond is set by the Court and will depend on the extent of P's net assets, income and outgoings and the level of experience of the deputy. An annual premium is usually payable from P's funds to cover this important insurance against the deputy 'turning bad' (unless P's assets are limited, in which case a one-off premium will be required).

What are the key problems areas?

These are examples of events which might raise concerns about whether the attorney's powers are being used properly.

Dealing with complaints about mental capacity

When a donor is unwell, or losing their mental capacity, family members who are not appointed as attorneys might sometimes try to make complaints on the donor's behalf. This could be because they believe that someone has misled the donor – by mis-selling an investment, for example. They might also object to the actions of the attorneys themselves.

Family disputes are difficult to resolve, as banks are only able to provide information to their customers or their official representatives. The same rules apply to people who bring their complaints to us.

Though a financial business should not act on unproven allegations made by other family members, they do have a duty of care to their customer. So, if the business thinks a power of attorney is being abused, they should report it to the relevant authority. They might also decide to refuse to carry out some instructions – like transferring of money from the donor to the attorney's account.

Excessive gifts [31]

Whilst attorneys can make gifts to people related to or connected with the donor, including themselves, these gifts should only be on customary occasions (for example birthdays, Christmas, etc) and should not be unreasonably large. The gifts should also not be disproportionate to the pattern of giving the donor did when they had capacity.

One of the consequences of an Attorney exceeding his or her authority could be realised at the time of dealing with an individual's estate. At that time, the Revenue will ask to see a copy of the Power of Attorney and will then look to see what gifts have been declared being made during the last seven years.

If the Donor had lost capacity and gifts were continuing to be made the

[31] There is some useful guidance here: https://www.gov.uk/government/publications/public-guardian-practice-note-gifts/public-guardian-practice-note-pn7-giving-gifts-web-version

Revenue may argue that the gifts are void and the value should be aggregated to the estate, with a result that the additional Inheritance Tax will be payable, plus there will be the potential for interest and penalties.

Matters could be even worse if there is evidence that there is a general deficiency in a Donor's funds because an Attorney has been withdrawing excessive sums from his or her account. In the case of R v TJC [2015] EWCA the Court of Appeal (Criminal Division) held that in such circumstances the Attorney would be guilty of an abuse of position under Section 4 of the Fraud Act 2006.

In this case the withdrawals being made by the Attorney were unreasonably high given the needs of the Donor. The conclusion was that the Attorney could not have been acting honesty when managing the affairs of the Donor.

It is easy to believe that as an Attorney, you are, in effect, standing in the same shoes as the Donor, and can act as he or she would do.

It is important for the Attorneys to remember that they must always act in the best interest of the Donor.

An attorney needs to take particular care if he or she is thinking of accepting a gift from the person's estate.

If one does accept a gift, the Court of Protection can look carefully at whether the person had capacity and may decide the attorney went beyond authority.

In the case of PG v DH [2014] EWCOP 15 (15 July 2014), Senior Judge Lush decided that the facts pointed to the 'donor' of a power of attorney (the legal term for the person who made it) lacking capacity to agree to a loan her son had taken out on her property. In this case, the donor's loan counted as a gift to her son.

Senior Judge Lush commented that:

... even if VH had the capacity to make the gift, it was reprehensible [wrong] of him [the attorney] to have accepted it... and shows that when faced with a conflict between his interests and his mother's, he would place his own interests first.

Loan applications or credit cards taken out in the donor's name

This could raise concerns about potential misuse of the attorney's powers, particularly if the donor does not benefit from the loans or credit cards. In Re Harcourt,[32] Mrs Harcourt's daughter became an attorney after her mother lost capacity.

Suspicions were raised when the care home manager became aware of letters about bank loans and credit card applications being taken out by the daughter in her mother's name. The matter was consequently investigated, and it was revealed that the daughter had abused her powers of attorney to make personal financial gains.

High risk investments or investment in a business the attorney owns or has an interest in

Before an attorney invests it is worth considering:

Check your LPA, EPA or court order first as there may be restrictions or clauses about investments or how you can use the person's money.

If you want to do something that's restricted the attorney should apply to the Court of Protection for permission. This will happen if you want to:

- invest a substantial amount of the person's money, particularly where the person had previously chosen to hold money in cash
- use the person's money to invest in your own business, a family member or friend
- You may need to include evidence such as financial statements and documented advice from a financial adviser with your application.

---

[32] Re Harcourt [2012] WTLR 1779

In addition, the attorney needs to

- Think about the person's current and future financial needs
- If possible, ask the person's opinion and collect financial information (also known as a financial fact find) for your plan. You should consider:
- their age, health and average life expectancy
- their current income and outgoings and how these may change
- whether their income will cover what they will spend on living
- how much the total assets are worth
- the cost of their care and accommodation
- whether they own property and what will happen to it, the costs of insurance, bills and maintenance
- other financial plans in place, any fixed term savings and maturity dates
- whether any major items of expenditure are anticipated
- whether any gifts or payments to dependants are likely to be made (this may involve an application to the court for permission)[33]
- whether you need to keep any funds in reserve for emergencies

The issue of investments was considered in the Court of Protection No. 12228697 Buckley v The Public Guardian.

The Senior Judge in the Court of Protection, Denzil Lush, stated that he

[33] https://www.gov.uk/guidance/investing-for-someone-as-their-attorney-or-deputy

wished to use this case to discuss the responsibilities of an attorney acting under an LPA when investing donor's funds.

"There are two common misconceptions when it comes to investments. The first is that attorneys acting under an LPA can do whatever they like with the donors' funds. And the second is that attorneys can do whatever the donors could – or would – have done personally, if they had the capacity to manage their property and financial affairs."

"Managing your own money is one thing. Managing someone else's money is an entirely different matter."

Attorneys hold a fiduciary position, which imposes a number of duties on them. Like trustees and other fiduciaries, they must exercise such care and skill as is reasonable in the circumstances when investing the donor's assets and this duty of care is even greater where attorneys hold themselves out as having specialist knowledge or experience. Although it does not expressly apply to attorneys, the Trustee Act 2000, section 4, requires trustees to have regard to what are known as the "standard investment criteria" when exercising any power of investment. There are two standard criteria, namely:

(1) the suitability of the investments; and

(2) the need to diversify the investments, in so far as it is appropriate in the circumstances.

Trustees are also required to review the investments from time to time and consider whether, having regard to the standard investment criteria, they should be varied.

Section 5 of the Trustee Act requires trustees, before exercising any powers of investment or reviewing the investments, to obtain and consider proper advice about the way in which, having regard to the standard investment criteria, their power should be exercised. In this context,

"proper advice" means the advice of a person who is reasonably believed by the trustee to be qualified to give it by his ability in and practical experience of financial and other matters relating to the proposed investment. There is an exception to this general rule, and trustees need not obtain such advice if they reasonably conclude that it is unnecessary or inappropriate to do so.

Two of the most important factors when considering the suitability of investments are the donor's age and life expectancy. Judge Lush pointed out that most donors are older people. Their average age is 80 years and 11 months, and, in this respect Miss Buckley, who was 81½, was a typical LPA donor.

ON LPAs if things go wrong

If the donor has sufficient capacity, they can cancel the LPA by signing a Deed of Revocation and notifying the attorney.

If the donor does not have capacity, you can contact the Office of the Public Guardian in the first instance and ask them to investigate the concerns.

If you have sufficient evidence regarding the abuse, you could make an application to the Court of Protection for an order that the LPA is cancelled and a deputy is instead appointed to manage the vulnerable person's finances. It is advisable to seek legal advice before court proceedings are started."

Applications for permission to make gifts

Attorneys and deputies have limited powers by which they can make gifts, or an application can be made to the Court of Protection for approval of a more substantial gift.

Applications for permission for property transactions

Attorneys and deputies may have the authority to sell the property belonging to the person lacking capacity. However, on occasion an application to the Court of Protection is required to obtain approval for such a transaction. This could be because the sale is at below market value or because a family member wants to buy it.

Statutory wills

If a person does not have the necessary testamentary capacity to make a will, then the court can make an order authorising a person to execute a will on their behalf.

The court will consider what would be in the best interests of the person and this includes how they would be remembered after their death.

When a person has lost the capacity to make a will and it is considered necessary to make a will, an application needs to be made asking the court of protection to authorise the execution of that will. An attorney or a deputy cannot execute a will without the Court of protection's approval.

In what circumstances will a statutory will be made?

- the vulnerable person has never made a will before
- the estate has reduced in value
- the estate has increased in value, for example, because of compensation awarded
- tax planning purposes
- a beneficiary (or beneficiaries) under an existing will has passed away
- a beneficiary under an existing will has already received substantial gifts, and the will should be adjusted

Overall, The Court of Protection is most likely to allow a statutory will if the person who lacks capacity has never made a will, or if there has been a significant change in their circumstances.

What are the legal variables to consider?

Prior to the Mental Capacity Act 2005, judges applied the substituted judgement test. In other words, the judge would assess what the vulnerable person would have done, had they had a brief lucid interval at the time the will was made.

However, this test is no longer heavily relied upon. The court of protection is now required to apply an objective test to assess whether the proposed statutory will is in the vulnerable person's best interests.

When considering a statutory will application, the court of protection will try to encourage the vulnerable person to participate, and will look at the factors listed in section 4 of the Mental Capacity Act 2005, such as:

The vulnerable person's past and present wishes and feelings (and any relevant written statement made by the vulnerable person when he had capacity).

The beliefs and values that would be likely to influence the vulnerable person's decision if they had capacity.

The other factors that the vulnerable person would be likely to consider if they were able to do so.

Furthermore, the Court of Protection may consider the views of those who are engaged in caring for the vulnerable person, along with the views of the attorney chosen by the vulnerable person, or the view of the deputy appointed for the vulnerable person by the court of protection, as to what would be in that vulnerable person's best interests.

It was held in the case of Re P [2009][34] that for many people, it is in their best interests that they be remembered with affection by their family and as having done 'the right thing' by their will.

However, recently there have been differing views expressed as to the relevance of the vulnerable person 'having done the right thing' by their will.

---

[34] In re P (Statutory Will): ChD 9 Feb 2009

Balancing wishes and best interests

A vulnerable person's known wishes and feelings will be of great importance. However, they are not paramount.

There is no hierarchy between the factors listed in section 4 of the Mental Capacity Act 2005. The weight to be attached to the various factors, including the vulnerable person's wishes, will depend largely on the individual circumstances of the case.

Ultimately, the Court of Protection must be convinced that authorising the execution of a statutory will is in the vulnerable person's best interests.

Challenging a LPA

The Court of Protection has power to consider "any questions relating to whether the power has been revoked or has otherwise end" (MCA 2005, s 22 (2) (b).

The Public Guardian may apply to the Court of Protection in serious cases (MCA Code of Practice 7.72) where the donor may have been subject to abuse or where there is a report that he donor may have been subject to undue influence or fraud in the creation of the power of the LPA.

Where it is satisfied that an attorney proposes to behave, has behaved, in a way that contravenes the donor's authority or is not in the donor's best interests, the court has discretion if another attorney is authorised to act jointly and severally can continue to act or the terms of the power allow for the appointment of a replacement attorney, to partially revoke the power as far as it relates the appointment of that attorney (MCA 2005 s 22 (5)).

The court can only exercise its power to revoke, or partially revoke, the power if the donor lacks capacity to revoke for him/herself. (MCA ss 22 (4) (b).

The Code of Practice at 7.72 states the Court:

> *Might then consider whether the authority previously given to attorney can be managed by:*

- *The court making a single decision*
- *Appointing a deputy*

Grounds for revoking an LPA

Under section 22(3) of the Mental Capacity Act 2005, the Court of Protection may revoke a LPA if it is satisfied that:

- fraud or undue pressure was used to induce the Donor to create the LPA; or
- the attorney of the LPA:
    - has behaved, or is behaving, in a way that contravenes his authority or is not in the Donor's best interests; or
    - proposes to behave in a way that would contravene his authority or would not be in the Donor's best interests.

Revoking an LPA is a serious step and the Court of Protection will look at all the circumstances, including the gravity of the offending or prospective behaviours. The Court will also consider whether it is necessary and proportionate to revoke an LPA and ultimately, whether the revocation would be in the Donor's best interests.

The following cases show the approach taken by the Court of Protection in deciding on revocation.

The Public Guardian v CS & PL [2015] EWCOP30

The Donor, EL, was diagnosed with vascular dementia in 2009 and appointed her two children, CS, and PL, as her attorneys with the power to act jointly in relation to the sale of her house and jointly and severally for all other decisions. The LPA was registered on 12 July 2010.

The attorneys' relationship broke down due to differing views on who should control EL's finances. They each made complaints to the Office of the Public Guardian and accused each other of misconduct. This led to PL making an application to the Court of Protection in December 2012 to revoke the LPA and for PL to be appointed as sole deputy for EL's finances. By that time, it was apparent that EL had lost the capacity to revoke her LPA.0000

It became clear to Senior Judge Lush that the LPA was not functioning properly due to the animosity between the attorneys and the refusal to respect the Schedule of Agreed Responsibilities. They had also delegated their responsibilities to their father.

In addition, the Judge was of the view that the attorneys made gifts to themselves from EL's funds which were far more than what they could do under section 12 of the Mental Capacity Act 2005. As a result, the Judge was satisfied that both attorneys behaved in a way that contravened their authority and was not in EL's best interests. The Judge ordered the revocation of the LPA and invited a panel deputy to apply to be appointed as EL's deputy for property and affairs.

A subsequent case regarding the revocation of LPAs followed only a month later and was heard by the same Judge.

Re GM [2013] [35]

Senior Judge Lush set out the parameters of "reasonable" gifting by Deputies. This case clarifies that the authority of deputies and attorneys to make gifts is limited without the court's consent. Re GM is a clear example of financial abuse by joint deputies that did not go unnoticed by the Office of the Public Guardian (OPG). One of the main jobs of the OPG is to supervise deputies appointed by the Court of Protection and it is reassuring to know that the OPG will notice such cases of excessive expenditure and refer the matter to the Court of Protection.

In Re GM, the judge found that the deputies were personally liable to G's estate and were ordered to repay £205,000. The joint deputyship appointments were revoked. The judge ordered that somebody 'with experience of unjust enrichment and restitution' be appointed in their place. In other words, a professional deputy should be appointed who

[35] Re GM: MJ v JM The Public Guardian [2013] EWCOP 2966.

could take the necessary legal action against the former deputies to enforce the court's order for repayment.

Legal Options

The key objective for Court of Protection lawyers and their clients will be in to stop the abuse and then give consideration to whether or not any remedies need to be sought to rectify the consequences of the abuse.

For probate practitioners, the main issue will be whether or not any proceedings should be brought to recover the proceeds of financial abuse in the interests of maximising the deceased person's estate or enabling a beneficiary to make a claim.

Court of Protection

Considerations are likely to arise as to whether or not an attorney or deputy needs to be removed and a deputy appointed in their stead in most cases where financial abuse is being perpetrated against a person without the capacity to manage their affairs.

The statutory jurisdiction for the removal of an attorney appointed by EPA is found in paragraph 16 of Schedule 4 MCA 2005. The "misconduct" ground for revocation is in paragraph 16(4)(g). The Court must direct the Public Guardian to cancel the registration of an EPA "on being satisfied that, having regard to all the circumstances, and in particular the attorney's relationship to or connection with the donor, the attorney is unsuitable to be the donor's attorney".

The statutory jurisdiction for the removal of an attorney appointed by LPA is found in section 22 of the MCA. The Court of Protection may direct that an instrument purporting to be an LPA is not to be registered or that it is to revoked (if P lacks capacity to do so), where the execution or creation of the LPA has been procured by fraud or undue pressure (s23(4)(a)) or where the donee has behaved or is proposing to behave in a way that would contravene his authority or is not, or would not be, in P's best interests (s23(4)(b)).

The jurisdiction in relation to the appointment, removal or supervision of deputies is derived from section 16 of the MCA.

Chancery Proceedings

It may also be appropriate to consider an action for breach of fiduciary duty, negligence, or a claim for restitution on the basis that the attorney has been unjustly enriched through misuse of the donor's funds. This typically happens after the Deceased has died and you are involved in an action for someone who has suffered financial loss due to the conduct of the attorney though legal action may be brought both in the lifetime of the victim and after their death.

There are a variety of civil actions that may be appropriate in circumstances of financial abuse including:4

- Set aside on the grounds of lack of capacity: The test for mental capacity for an inter vivos gift has been stated in Re Beaney [1978] 2 All ER 595 as follows: "the principle is that the mental capacity required by the law in respect of any instrument is relative to the particular transaction which is being effected by means of the instrument, and may be described as the capacity to understand the nature of that transaction when it is explained. "

- Breach of fiduciary duty / breach of trust: in circumstances where a person has assumed a responsibility for assisting another with their finances pursuant to a power of attorney or as a court appointed deputy, the courts have recognised that a fiduciary relationship arises.[36]

- Undue influence: Undue influence is an equitable doctrine which provides that transactions (including gifts and contracts) may be

[36] No period of limitation applies to an action by a beneficiary under a trust in respect of any fraud or fraudulent breach of trust to which the trustee was a party, or to recover from the trustee trust property (or the proceeds of trust property) in the possession of the trustee (section 21(1) of the Limitation Act 1980) (a time limit of six years will apply in the case of non-fraudulent breaches of trust or fiduciary duty).

set aside in circumstances where the transaction has been procured by conduct, which, whilst falling short of actual fraud, consists of the exercise of an unfair advantage, typically by a party in a position of power, influence or trust, over the other party to the transaction. The rational of the doctrine then is to protect vulnerable parties from exploitation by people in whom they repose trust and confidence. It is not a necessary ingredient of the doctrine that misconduct on the part of the stronger party should be demonstrated. Where undue influence is found, the transaction in question may be set aside.

- Morally culpable behaviour: The weakness of one party has to have been exploited by the other in some morally culpable manner. Overreaching or oppressive result: The resulting transaction must be not merely hard or improvident, but overreaching or oppressive.

Approaching Cases

Attorneys under an LPA are expected to act in the Donor's best interests always and follow the Code of Practice. If they cannot be trusted to act in the Donor's best interests, recent case law has shown that the Public Guardian and the Court of Protection will intervene, and the LPA may be revoked and cancelled in some circumstances.

TIP

A very useful piece of legislation is the Mentality Capacity Code and as a lawyer I like to remind errant attorneys of their breaches.

Principles and best interests

7.53 Attorneys must act in accordance with the Act's statutory principles (section 1) and in the best interests of the donor (the steps for working out best interests are set out in section 4). In particular, attorney s must consider whether the donor has capacity to make the decision for themselves. If not, they should consider whether the donor is likely to regain capacity to make the decision in the future. If so, it may be possible to delay the decision until the donor can make it.

What are an attorney's other duties?

7.58 An attorney appointed under an LPA is acting as the chosen agent of the donor and therefore, under the law of agency, the attorney has certain duties towards the donor. An attorney takes on a role which carries a great deal of power, which they must use carefully and responsibly. They have a duty to:

- *apply certain standards of care and skill (duty of care) when making decisions*
- *carry out the donor's instructions*
- *not take advantage of their position and not benefit themselves, but benefit the donor (fiduciary duty)*
- *not delegate decisions, unless authorised to do so*
- *act in good faith*
- *respect confidentiality*
- *comply with the directions of the Court of Protection*
- *not give up the role without telling the donor and the court.*

In relation to property and affairs LPAs, they have a duty to:

- *keep accounts*
- *keep the donor's money and property separate from their own.*

Duty of care

7.59 'Duty of care' means applying a certain standard of care and skill – depending on whether the attorney is paid for their services or holds relevant professional qualifications.

- *Attorneys who are not being paid must apply the same care, skill and diligence they would use to make decisions about their own life. An attorney who claims to have particular skills or qualifications must show greater skill in those particular areas than someone who does not make such claims.*

- *If attorneys are being paid for their services, they should demonstrate a higher degree of care and skill.*

- *Attorneys who undertake their duties in the course of their professional work (such as solicitors or corporate trustees) must display professional competence and follow their profession's rules and standards.*

Mental Capacity Act Code of Practice Fiduciary duty

7.60 A fiduciary duty means attorneys must not take advantage of their position. Nor should they put themselves in a position where their personal interests' conflict with their duties. They also must not allow any other influences to affect the way in which they act as an attorney. Decisions should always benefit the donor, and not the attorney. Attorneys must not profit or get any personal benefit from their position, apart from receiving gifts where the Act allows it, whether or not it is at the donor's expense.

Duty of good faith

7.63 Acting in good faith means acting with honesty and integrity. For example, an attorney must try to make sure that their decisions do not go against a decision the donor made while they still had capacity

(unless it would be in the donor's best interests to do so).

It is often difficult to find specific evidence in these circumstances as to what the attorney has done with missing funds, and it is useful to know that even when it comes to meeting the onerous burden of proving fraud, it is not always necessary to determine exactly what the funds have been spent on.

This is demonstrated by the case of R v TJC [2015] EWCA Crim 1276. In this case it was held that it is possible to bring a charge against an attorney if there is 'abuse of position' under Section 4 of the Fraud Act

2006. [37] The Court held that the circumstances would need to show that there is evidence of a general deficiency in the donor's funds as a result of withdrawals made by an attorney. In this case, the Court of Appeal held that it was not necessary for the prosecution to present evidence of specific fraudulent transactions, i.e. identifying each withdrawal against expenditure. What was sufficient in this case was demonstrating that the total value of withdrawals by the Attorney (totalling approximately £75,000), exceeded the reasonable sums that would have been incurred over specific periods in providing for the donor given their needs. In this case, although it was accepted that some of the funds were spent on the donor, the Attorney had been spending "sums to such a degree and in such high quantities in certain given months that she could not possibly have been acting honestly".

In general, where there is suspected financial abuse by an attorney, the Office of the Public Guardian ("OPG") should be informed immediately.

TIP

It may be less expensive for our clients to just refer to the OPG, but you are handing power to a third party and they will not investigate cases post death. The question of whether or not proceedings should be issued is a difficult one for both probate and Court of Protectionl lawyers. In both instances, you will be asking yourself the key question of whether or not the funds you are administering on behalf of another should be expended on pursuing proceedings.

---

[37] In an initial letter of claim, threatening criminal proceedings and quoting legislation and case law can be a useful step but you must ensure that you have evidence to back it up. Much of my work involving financial abuse involves the instruction of forensic accountant and this is often a point of call prior to approaching the fraudulent attorney..

On behalf of the Claimant

First Statement of XXX

Exhibits 5 marked as XX

Date Signed

IN THE HIGH COURT OF JUSTICE
Claim No

BUSINESS AND PROPERTY COURTS OF ENGLAND AND WALES

PROPERTY, TRUSTS AND PROBATE LIST (ChD)

IN THE MATTER OF THE ESTATE OF xxx

BETWEEN

MR

Claimant

And

MRS

Defendant(1)

MRS

Defendant(2)

STATEMENT OF MR X

I YJ X unit Z

1. The background to this matter is further to my father passing away on xxx, my mother, Mrs AZ, (The Deceased) set up a trust to deal with her financial affairs created a Trust which I am a beneficiary in, a copy of which is exhibited in XX.

2. Since the Trust were set up in xx, the First Defendant has been the lead Trustee and exercised primary control of the money and the running of the Deceased's affairs particularly in the latter years of the Deceased's life. I am concerned that the First Defendant has not acted correctly with her duties as Trustee of the trust and may be taking money out of the Trust.

3. Since xx, I have instructed solicitors who have been corresponding with the Defendant to ensure that she discloses the Trust documents, financial information such as accounts of the Trusts and its bank statements. My solicitors have found the Defendant to be persistently evasive and grudging in making any form of disclosure and payments to me via my solicitors. In particular, I refer the Court to the bundle of documents in exhibit before me within xxx which contains the key correspondence between my solicitors and the Defendant together with some correspondence with Mrs Q and her solicitors.

4. The difficulties which I have experienced in eliciting disclosure of trust documents, payments and information on bank statements is shown in a Letter Before Action which my solicitors wrote dated XX in document number 3 and 4 of exhibit XX.

5. It is clear that the Defendant accepts there is a financial liability to me, she has provided a one page financial summary and some bank statements relating to the Trusts but is maintaining her pattern of being evasive and often covering issues which have no relevance. And, most significantly, she is refusing to disclose information prior to xx so that I do not have a full picture of what is going on before this date. I refer the Court to the emails of the First Defendant dated xx and xx which shows this latest impasse and the effective refusal of the Defendant to disclose bank statements and accounts prior to XXX which I am legally entitled to.

6. As a consequence, I seek a Court order that the First Defendant disclose all documents and financial records in respect of the interest in possession settlement dated 18 December 2000.

7. I believe the facts stated in this witness statement are true.

Signed ....

Dated..

CHAPTER SEVEN

MENTAL CAPACITY

Mental health/lack of capacity

One of the most difficult areas for solicitors is raising the issue of a client's mental health or a concern regarding their capacity to provide you with instructions.

It is of course a highly sensitive issue, and many sufferers of mental ill health have little or no insight into their own difficulties.

Mental capacity is assessed under the MCA 2005, which states that a person must be assumed to have capacity unless it is established that they lack capacity (s1(1) MCA 2005).

Whether a person has capacity is determined by the court and although it is likely to place considerable weight on medical opinion, this is not conclusive.

The court will look at all evidence, medical and otherwise.

We now turn to some key issues which elderly practitioners may face namely:

1. Advance decisions
2. Deprivation of Liberty Safeguards (DoLS)

Advance decisions

What is an advance decision?

An advance decision (sometimes known as an advance decision to refuse treatment, or a living will) is a decision one can make now to refuse a specific type of treatment at some time in the future.[38]

It lets ones' family, carers and health professionals know whether you want to refuse specific treatments in the future. This means these people will know your wishes if you are unable to make or communicate those decisions yourself.

One can only make an advance decision if:

- you have the capacity to make those decisions now
- you are an adult (at least 18 years old)

The treatments one is deciding to refuse must all be named in the advance decision.

One may want to refuse a treatment in some situations but not others.

If this is the case, one needs to be clear about all the circumstances in which one want to refuse this treatment.

Definition of an advance decision

An "advance decision" has a specific statutory meaning, provided for in s.24(1 MCA), namely:

> *"a decision made by a person ('P') after he has reached 18 and when he has capacity to do so, that if–*
>
> *(a) later and in such circumstances as he may specify, a specified treatment is proposed to be carried out or continued by a person providing health care for him, and*
>
> *(b) at that time, he lacks capacity to consent to the carrying out or continuation of the treatment,*
>
> *the specified treatment is not to be carried out or continued."*

---

[38] https://compassionindying.org.uk/library/ has some excellent resources on the subject.

The Act does not specify the terms in which a person is required to set out their decision am s.24(6) makes clear that a decision can be regarded as "specifying a treatment or circumstances even though it is expressed in layman's terms" (s.24(2)).

Chapter 9 of the Code of Practice accompanying the MCA 2005 suggests that it is helpful to include the following information:

- full details of its maker, including date of birth, home address and any distinguishing features (so that – for instance – an unconscious person might be identified)
- the name and address of general practitioner and whether they have a copy
- a statement that the document should be used if the maker lacks capacity to make treatment decisions
- a clear statement of the decision, the treatment to be refused and the circumstances in which the decision will apply
- the date the document was written (or reviewed); and
- the person's signature (or that of the person signing in their presence on their behalf) and the signature of a witness (if there is one).

These provisions of the Code of Practice have been the subject of specific judicial endorsement.

The Practicalities of Advance Decision[39]

With an advance decision, one can refuse a treatment that could potentially keep the person alive (known as life-sustaining treatment). This includes treatments such as ventilation and cardiopulmonary resuscitation (CPR), which may be used if you cannot breathe by yourself or if your

[39] There has been very little case law connected with advance decisions regarding advance decisions since the implementation of the MCA.

heart stops.[40]

An advance decision needs to be:

- written down
- signed by the person making it
- signed by a witness

The charity Compassion in Dying has an advance decision form you can fill in online or by hand, with suggestions for things to think about. You need to register (for free) on the website before you can see the form.

It is legally binding if it complies with the Mental Capacity Act is valid applies to the situation.

It needs to be signed and witnessed if one is choosing to refuse life-sustaining treatment. In this case, the advance decision must be written down, and both you and a witness must sign it.

You must also include a statement that the advance decision applies even if your life is at risk.

Everyone has the right to refuse CPR if they wish, e.g., one can make it clear to your medical team that you do not want to have CPR if you stop breathing or your heart stops beating.

This is known as a "do not attempt cardiopulmonary resuscitation" (DNACPR) decision or DNACPR order. Once a DNACPR decision is made, it is put in your medical records, usually on a special form that

[40] It was reported in 2017 that the family of Brenda Grant received compensation from the NHS in respect of the way in which Brenda had been treated prior to her death. Brenda had made an advanced directive in which she was clear that she would not want to be artificially fed under certain circumstances. The hospital had not discovered the document in a thick bundle of medical documents and none of the family knew about it. The intervention of the GP who did know of its existence at a late stage meant that her wishes were honoured.

health professionals will recognise.

How Does One Change An Advance Decision?

You can change your advance decision at any time, and the Mental Capacity Act does not have a particular way for you to do it.

If you want to change your advance decision, you should do the following:

Do it in writing.

Cancel and destroy your old advance decision and make a new one if you can. This helps to avoid any confusion as to which advance decision applies.

Tell other people such as your family or close friends, GP, carer or relevant healthcare professionals that you have made a new advance decision and that you wish to destroy the old one.

If your advance decision includes a refusal of life-saving treatment, you must change your advance decision in writing. If you want to cancel your refusal of lifesaving treatment, and are unable to do it in writing at the time, you should tell healthcare professionals who are treating you and anyone close to you as soon as possible, and try to get it put in your medical notes. Then change your advance decision in writing or make a new one as soon as you can.

It is important to make any changes to your advance decision as clear as possible because:

by the time you have lost capacity and health professionals are trying to follow your advance decision, you will probably not be able to answer questions about it

it will be difficult to follow your advance decision if there is confusion around it or if it is not clear whether you have altered it.

Terminology advance statement v advance decision

An advance statement is a written statement that sets down your preferences, wishes, beliefs and values regarding your future care.

The aim is to provide a guide to anyone who might have to make decisions in your best interest if you have lost the capacity to make decisions or to communicate them.

It can cover any aspect of your future health or social care. This could include:

- how you want any religious or spiritual beliefs you hold to be reflected in your care

- where you would like to be cared for – for example, at home or in a hospital, a nursing home, or a hospice

- how you like to do things – for example, if you prefer a shower instead of a bath, or like to sleep with the light on

- concerns about practical issues – for example, who will look after your dog if you become ill

It is not legally binding but anyone who is making decisions about your care must take it into account

By contrast an advance decision is legally binding.

One can have both an Advance Decision (Living Will) and a Lasting Power of Attorney for Health and Welfare (LPA).

If one does, the one that you made more recently will take priority when a decision needs to be made about your treatment and care.

For example:

If you make an LPA after making an Advance Decision your attorney will be able to override what's written in your Advance Decision if, when you made the LPA, you gave them the power to make the decision in question (for example, by choosing that they can make decisions about life-sustaining treatment).

If you make an Advance Decision after making an LPA, your attorney will not be able to override what is written in your Advance Decision. In this situation, if a decision needs to be made about something that you have not detailed in your Advance Decision, then your attorney will still be able to act on your behalf.

If you have both an Advance Decision and an LPA, one must make sure that you tell your attorney about your Advance Decision and give them a copy.

For those advising upon the making of an advance decision, it is always vitally important to bear in mind that there is an alternative to such a decision which has the power to avoid at least some of the difficult pitfalls outlined above.

A lasting power of attorney can be created with authority for the person chosen as donee to take health care decisions, including as to the refusal of life-sustaining treatment.

Such authority must be expressly included in the instrument8 and is subject to any conditions or restrictions in the instrument.

Once registered, an appropriately worded LPA will put the donee in the shoes of the donor in respect of treatment decisions the donor no longer has the capacity to take subject to two provisos:

- where the person has lost capacity to revoke an LPA, an LPA can be revoked by the Court of Protection if the Court is satisfied that: (1) the donee has behaved, or are behaving, in a way that contravenes their authority or is not in P's best interests; or (2) the donee proposes to behave in a way which in a way that would contravene their authority or is not in P's best interests.

- the Court can also give directions with respect to decisions which the donee of an LPA has authority to make and which P lacks the capacity to make

Dealing with disagreements about an advance decision

The senior doctor or healthcare professional treating you is responsible for deciding whether there is a valid, applicable advance decision related to the current situation.

If there is a dispute between professionals or between professionals and family members, this responsible person must consider all available evidence.

This means consulting relevant colleagues and others familiar with you, such as your GP. If they must make an urgent decision without delay, a doctor can apply to the Court of Protection.

The Court of Protection can make a declaration on:

- whether you have mental capacity to make the decision at the time it must be made (if you do, the advance decision does not come into play)
- whether the advance decision is valid
- whether the advance decision is applicable to the treatment and circumstances.

The Court of Protection cannot overturn a valid and applicable advance decision. It cannot order treatment to be provided, if it has been refused in a valid advance decision. For more on applying to the Court of Protection.[41]

---

41 MCA Co9.67 The Court of Protection can make a decision where there is genuine doubt or disagreement about an advance decision's existence, validity or applicability. But the court does not have the power to overturn a valid and applicable advance decision. The court has a range of powers (sections 16–17)to resolve disputes concerning the personal care and medical treatment of a person who lacks capacity (see chapter 8). It can decide whether:

• a person has capacity to accept or refuse treatment at the time it is proposed • an advance decision to refuse treatment is valid • an advance decision is applicable to the proposed treatment in the current circumstances. 9.69 While the court decides, healthcare professionals can provide life-sustaining treatment or treatment to stop a serious deterioration in their condition. The court has emergency procedures which operate 24 hours a day to deal with urgent cases quickly. See chapter

If there is any doubt or disagreement over whether an advance decision exists, is valid or is applicable to a treatment, an application can be made to the Court of Protection for it to make declarations under the provisions of ss.26(4)(a)-(c) respectively.

While a decision is being sought, those treating the person concerned are entitled to take nothing in the apparent advance decision as preventing them providing life-sustaining treatment or doing any act they reasonably believe to be necessary to prevent a serious deterioration in that person's condition (s.26(5)).

The importance of bringing matters relating to the existence, validity and/or applicability of an advance decision to Court as quickly as possible was emphasised in the cases of A Local Authority v E and X Primary Care Trust v XB:

2. Key Principles of Deprivation of Liberty Safeguards (DoLS)

- The Mental Capacity Act 2005 includes the Deprivation of Liberty Safeguards (DoLS) – a set of checks that aims to make sure that any care that restricts a person's liberty is both appropriate and in their best interests.

- The Deprivation of Liberty Safeguards are an amendment to the Mental Capacity Act 2005. They apply in England and Wales only.

- The Mental Capacity Act allows restraint and restrictions to be used – but only if they are in a person's best interests.

- Extra safeguards are needed if the restrictions and restraint used will deprive a person of their liberty. These are called the Deprivation of Liberty Safeguards.

- The Deprivation of Liberty Safeguards can only be used if the person will be deprived of their liberty in a care home or hospital. In other

8 for guidance on applying to the court.

settings the Court of Protection can authorise a deprivation of liberty.

- Care homes or hospitals must ask a local authority if they can deprive a person of their liberty. This is called requesting a standard authorisation.

- There are six assessments which have to take place before a standard authorisation can be given.

- If a standard authorisation is given, one key safeguard is that the person has someone appointed with legal powers to represent them. This is called the relevant person's representative and will usually be a family member or friend.

- Other safeguards include rights to challenge authorisations in the Court of Protection, and access to Independent Mental Capacity Advocates (IMCAs).

The law

Article 5 of the Human Rights Act states that 'everyone has the right to liberty and security of person. No one shall be deprived of his or her liberty [unless] in accordance with a procedure prescribed in law'. The Deprivation of Liberty Safeguards is the procedure prescribed in law when it is necessary to deprive of their liberty a resident or patient who lacks capacity to consent to their care and treatment to keep them safe from harm.

The Supreme Court judgement in March 2014 called Cheshire West made reference to the 'acid test' to see whether a person is being deprived of their liberty, which consisted of two questions:

If someone is subject to that level of supervision, and is not free to leave, then it is likely that they are being deprived of their liberty. But even with the 'acid test' it can be difficult to be clear when the use of restrictions and restraint in someone's support crosses the line to depriving a person of their liberty. Each case must be considered on its own merits, but in addition to the two 'acid test' questions, if the following features are present, it would make sense to consider a deprivation of liberty application:

- frequent use of sedation/medication to control behaviour
- regular use of physical restraint to control behaviour
- the person concerned objects verbally or physically to the restriction and/or restraint
- objections from family and/or friends to the restriction or restraint
- the person is confined to a particular part of the establishment in which they are being cared for
- the placement is potentially unstable
- possible challenge to the restriction and restraint being proposed to the Court of Protection or the Ombudsman, or a letter of complaint or a solicitor's letter
- the person is already subject to a deprivation of liberty authorisation which is about to expire.

DoLS only apply for people in care homes and hospitals.

There is a separate system for people in 'supported living arrangements' – where people live and receive care in the community.

An assessment will decide whether the deprivation of liberty is allowed to happen or not.

A DoLS assessment will take place if a person with dementia is in a care home or hospital setting and it is felt that they are being, or will be, deprived of their liberty.

If the person with dementia is living in supported living, there is a different system for having a deprivation of liberty authorised. This is outlined towards the end of this page – see 'Supported living'.

Usually, the care provider – the care home or hospital – will request the DoLS assessment. In England, they would request the assessment from the local authority. In Wales, for assessments of people in care homes it would be the local authority, but for people in hospitals it would be the local health board.

If one feels that someone is being deprived of their liberty, you should speak to the person in charge of their care. In hospital this may be a doctor, nurse or administrator, and in residential care it will be the care home manager.

The first step is to talk about whether changes can be made to the way care is provided so that the person's freedom is not restricted. However, if the person in charge of their care believes that restricting the person's freedom is necessary to keep them safe, they must apply for a deprivation of liberty authorisation.

If they have not got an authorisation, and they do not think that an authorisation is necessary, you should talk to the local authority (or local health board in Wales). You should ask them to look into the person's care arrangements and carry out an assessment, if necessary.

With respect to DoLS assessments, they are carried out by at least two people. They are:

- the best interest's assessor
- the mental health assessor

They are appointed by the local authority (or health board), who must ensure that they have had the appropriate level of training and experience.

Generally, the best interest's assessor is a qualified social worker, nurse, occupational therapist or chartered psychologist. They must not be involved in the person's care or in making any other decisions about it. The mental health assessor must be a doctor who is able to assess whether a person has a 'mental disorder' (the term used in law to describe a set of mental health conditions, including dementia) and how a deprivation of liberty will affect their mental health.

What does the assessment involve?

There are six parts to the assessment. These are divided between the two assessors. Their job is to decide whether the person and the care that they receive meet the criteria for authorisation. The six parts are as follows:

- Age – Is the person aged 18 years or over?
- Mental health – Does the person have a 'mental disorder'?
- Mental capacity – Does the person lack 'capacity' (the ability) to make their own decisions about treatment or care in the place that is applying for the authorisation?
- Best interests – Is a deprivation of liberty taking place? If so, is it:
    - in the person's best interests?
    - needed to keep the person safe from harm?
    - a reasonable response to the likelihood of the person suffering harm (including whether there are any less restrictive options and if they are more appropriate)?
- Eligibility – Is the person already liable to detention under the Mental Health Act 1983, or would they meet the requirements for detention under this Act?
- No refusals – Does the authorisation contradict or conflict with any advance decision the person has made refusing treatment, or with any decisions made by, for example, a court-appointed deputy or someone with Lasting power of attorney?

If someone meets all the criteria, the assessors will report back to the local authority (or local health board) that the deprivation of liberty should be authorised, i.e., given the legal 'go ahead'.

When the criteria are not met -If the assessors decide that the person or the proposed care doesn't meet the criteria, they will inform the local authority (or local health board) of this and the reasons for it. The deprivation of liberty would then not be authorised, and it should not happen. What happens next will depend upon the reasons why the criteria were not met.

For example, if the assessment showed that the person has capacity to consent to and make the decision about their care and where they will live, they should be empowered to make their own decision, and this should be followed.

Urgent DoLS

In an emergency, or in situations where there is no time to go through the assessment process, the hospital or care home management can grant themselves an urgent DoLS authorisation. This is valid for seven days, but they must also apply for the normal DoLS assessment and authorisation at the same time. If the assessment has not been carried out in the following seven days and the deprivation of liberty is still needed, the urgent DoLS authorisation can be extended for a further seven days.

Before an urgent DoLS authorisation is given, steps should be taken to consult with a person's carers and family members.

Challenging A DoLS

Challenging an unauthorised deprivation of liberty any third party (e.g. a member of staff, family member, friend or carer) who thinks you are being deprived of your liberty without authorisation can: ask the care home or hospital to apply for authorisation, or to change the care regime so that you are not being deprived of your liberty if this is not done, apply to the supervisory body for an assessment of whether you are being deprived of your liberty.

This assessment must be carried out within seven calendar days.

If there is a deprivation of liberty the full assessment procedure must go ahead. They can write a letter or make a verbal request, but it is always useful to have written evidence confirming when the request was made. If they think an unauthorised deprivation of liberty is taking place and they raise this with the care home or hospital, they should expect them to deal with it urgently.

The Code states this usually means within 24 hours. The person appointed to assess whether a deprivation of liberty is taking place should consult the person who raised the concern, the person themselves and any friends and family. If there is no family or friend to consult, an IMCA must be appointed. An unauthorised deprivation of liberty can also be challenged at the Court of Protection.

Challenging an authorisation

The person being deprived of their liberty, their RPR or an IMCA can apply for an authorisation to be reviewed. If authorisation is given and it is not thought to be in the person's best interests, the supervisory body and managing authority should be asked for evidence of what alternatives to deprivation were considered and why they were rejected.

Taking a case to the Court of Protection

The Court of Protection was created by the Mental Capacity Act 2005 to oversee actions taken under the Act, including those relating to DoLS, and to resolve any disputes involving mental capacity. A case is usually only taken to the Court of Protection if it has not been possible to resolve the matter with the managing authority and supervising body, either by asking for an assessment to be carried out or a review of an existing authorisation.

This may be in form of a formal complaint. Due to the serious nature of depriving someone of their liberty, you should not delay involving the Court if a managing authority or supervisory body is not dealing with a request to assess or review urgently.

The following people can bring a case to the Court of Protection:

- the person who is being deprived of liberty, or at risk of deprivation

- an attorney under a Lasting Power of Attorney
- a Court of Protection appointed deputy
- a person named in an existing Court Order related to the application
  - the RPR (Relevant person's Representative)

With respect to dementia issues one may wish to complain to the Care Quality Commission (care homes) and for social services (Local Authority Social Services and National Health Services Complaints.

Another option is the Local Government Ombudsman.

Judicial Review

A last resort of dealing with elderly client law is to ensure that if you do take legal action it is a last resort and ultimately if you do go down this route it has a specific objective namely the achievement of the outcome that you want for your client.

One ultimate method is judicial review which is the procedure by which an individual can seek to challenge the policy, decision, action or failure to act of a public body.

Bodies which are amenable to judicial review include government departments, local authorities or other body exercising a public function such as a CCG or an NHS Trust.

Grounds of Judicial Review and Remedies

A challenge against a public body can be brought on a growing number of grounds.

The main grounds of challenge in most judicial review cases are the following:

- Irrationality / unreasonableness – unreasonableness is where the decision is so "outrageous" or "absurd" that no reasonable body of persons could have reached it.

- Illegality – this is where a public body: o acts outside of its powers. This is known as acting "ultra vires"; or acts in breach of a requirement under a particular statute.

- Procedural impropriety – this includes a duty to act in accordance with rules of natural justice and procedural fairness and follow procedural requirements. Specific grounds under this heading can include:

- Bias – both actual bias (very rare) and appearance of bias – as the law requires decision making both to be fair and to be seen to be fair.

- Fairness – at its most basic meaning that two like cases should be treated in the same way.

- Legitimate expectation – where a public body says that it will act in a particular way, that representation may give rise to a legitimate expectation that the public authority will do as it said it would and the court may enforce this.

- Breach of Human Rights – The vast majority of the rights contained in the European Convention on Human Rights are now part of English law as a result of the Human Rights Act 1998 and as a result it is unlawful for a public body not to act in accordance with those rights.

Judicial Reviews are heard in the Administrative Court, a part of the High Court, which sits in locations across the country.

Appeals in judicial review cases are heard by the Court of Appeal and then in the most important cases by the Supreme Court. Decisions of the Supreme Court trump all other decisions; decisions of the Court of Appeal trump those of the High Court.

If a judicial review challenge is successful, the court may:

- make a mandatory order (i.e., an order requiring the public body to do something);
- make a prohibiting order (i.e., an order preventing the public body from doing something);
- make a quashing order (i.e., an order quashing the public body' s decision); or
- issue a declaration – a way in which the court can state what the law is and how the public body has got it wrong without directly interfering with the decision. The public body will be expected to take necessary steps to act in accordance with the declaration.

The most common types of remedies are quashing orders and declarations. It is very rare that the court will make a mandatory order unless there is really only one lawful course of action open to the public body and it refuses to take that action voluntarily.

In addition, the court has powers to grant interim relief (requiring something to happen / not to happen pending a final decision). For example, in a case where a family are arguing that their child is not being provided with suitable social care and that the local authority are therefore acting unlawfully under s2 Chronically Sick and Disabled Persons Act 1970, the court might order that some social care provision should be put in place on an interim basis pending the final hearing of the claim.

Procedure and Time-limits

Examples of making an application for judicial review are where someone has dementia and a local authority have provided services which are inadequate

Before an application for judicial review can be issued, the claimant has to comply with the pre-action protocol which requires, where time permits, for the claimant to send a letter before claim and allow 14 days for a response.

The Claimant must then obtain "permission" from the court to bring the judicial review claim.

Permission is usually decided by a Judge considering the papers but sometimes an oral hearing is required. The test for permission is whether the claimant has an arguable case, and only once permission has been granted, can you proceed with the judicial review.

It is important to note that any judicial review challenge must be brought promptly and in any event within three months of the original decision being challenged.

The court has a discretion to extend time where it is fair and just to do so but it cannot be assumed that this will happen in any particular case. It is therefore important to consider at an early stage whether a formal complaint to the local authority and/or Ombudsman will provide a satisfactory remedy to the concerns or whether a legal challenge by way of a judicial review is more appropriate.

It is a discretionary remedy which even if the Court has decided that the public authority have acted poorly may not grant the relief sought. The area of law is complex and use of this method must be a last resort.

Reform

In July 2018, the government published a Mental Capacity (Amendment) Bill, which passed into law in May 2019. It replaces the Deprivation of Liberty Safeguards (DoLS) with a scheme known as the Liberty Protection Safeguards (although the term is not used in the Bill itself).[42]

Key features of the Liberty Protection Safeguards (LPS) include:

In line with the Law Commission's suggestion, they start at 16 years old.

---

[42] The context of the legal reform is here: https://www.lawcom.gov.uk/project/mental-capacity-and-deprivation-of-liberty/ The DoLS was considered over complex and the new legislation replaces the DoLS processes with a broader scheme called the LPS.

There is no statutory definition of a deprivation of liberty beyond that in the Cheshire West and Surrey Supreme Court judgement of March 2014 – the 'acid test'

Deprivations of liberty have to be authorised in advance by the 'responsible body'.

For NHS hospitals, the responsible body will be the 'hospital manager'.

For arrangements under Continuing Health Care outside of a hospital, the 'responsible body' will be their local CCG (or Health Board in Wales).

In all other cases – such as in care homes, supported living schemes etc. (including for self-funders), and private hospitals, the responsible body will be the local authority.

The new Act also broadens the scope to treat people, and deprive them of their liberty, in a medical emergency, without gaining prior authorisation.

The target date for implementation is 1 April 2022. Prior to this, following a 12-week consultation planned for 2021, both a single Mental Capacity Act and LPS Code of Practice, and regulations, will be laid before Parliament and subsequently published. The sector trusts this will bring clarity to some outstanding questions about how LPS will work in practice and the training and implementation required.

CHAPTER EIGHT

LPA, WILL AND PROBATE FRAUD

An understated (and growing) area of criminal activity focuses on LPA and probate fraud and there is good reason to do so.

According to a report by the Society of Trust and Estate Practitioners (STEP), the cost of probate fraud[43] is predicted to be in the region of £150 million, some £100 million in excess of what was previously estimated.

In 2017 retired Senior Judge Denzil Lush has said people should be far more aware of the risks and has vowed to never sign one himself.[44]

Mr Lush, the author of the definitive legal guide to this area, has dealt with in 6,000 power of attorney cases.

In a foreword to his book, he says the "lack of transparency causes suspicions and concerns which tend to rise in a crescendo and eventually explode" and the Ministry of Justice (MoJ) has been "disingenuous" in promoting them.

This is quite a strong and powerful rebuke of the LPA culture and with the rise of LPAs LPA and probate fraud is going to rise.

Lasting Power of Attorneys

At the LPA level recourse includes:

---

[43] https://www.thegazette.co.uk/all-notices/content/101098

[44] https://www.lawgazette.co.uk/law/i-would-never-sign-a-power-of-attorney-retired-judge/5062465.article

- Objecting[45]

You can object to the registration of a lasting power of attorney (LPA). You must tell the Office of the Public Guardian (OPG).

You may also have to tell the Court of Protection.

How you object depends on who you are and why you're objecting.

Object if you're the donor

Fill in the objection form (LPA006) and send it to OPG. The address is on the form.

Object if you're an attorney or 'person to be told'.

You'll receive a letter from the donor or one of their attorneys telling you they want to register the LPA. You can make a 'factual objection' or an objection on 'prescribed grounds'.

Factual objections

You can object if:

- the donor or an attorney has died
- the donor and an attorney were married or had a civil partnership but have divorced or ended the civil partnership
- an attorney doesn't have the mental capacity to be an attorney
- an attorney has chosen to stop acting (sometimes called 'disclaiming their appointment')

---

45 With respect to Enduring Power of Attorney (which are still valid legal documents), there are two ways to object – the one you use depends on whether you've received an official letter telling you someone wants to register the EPA. More practical information is provided at https://www.gov.uk/object-registration/enduring-power

- the donor or an attorney are bankrupt, interim bankrupt or subject to a Debt Relief Order (property and financial affairs attorneys only)

Fill in the objection form (LPA007) and send it to OPG. The address is on the form.

You must object within 3 weeks of being told about the registration.

Prescribed objections

You can object to the registration if you think:

- the LPA isn't legally correct
- you don't believe the donor had mental capacity to make a LPA
- the donor cancelled their LPA when they regained capacity
- there was fraud, e.g., someone faked the donor's signature
- the donor was pressured to make an LPA
- an attorney is acting against the donor's best interests

You'll need to be able to provide evidence to support any of these objections.

Fill in the:

- notification form (LPA008) and send it to OPG (the address is on the form)
- objection form (COP7), copy it and send both the original and the copy to the Court of Protection (the address is on the form)

It doesn't cost anything to object if you're an attorney or person to be told.

Make an objection if you're not an attorney or 'person to be told'

Fill in the objection form (COP1), copy it and send both the original and the copy to the Court of Protection.

Send a cheque for £400 made payable to 'HM Courts and Tribunals Service' with your forms.

Court of Protection
PO Box 70185
First Avenue House
42-49 High Holborn
London
WC1A 9JA

Get a reduction or exemption of the fee

You may not have to pay the fees if you're on means-tested benefits or a low income.

After you've sent the forms and any fees, you'll be contacted by OPG or the Court of Protection within 5 days. They'll tell you if:

- they're going to stop the registration
- there's going to be a hearing to discuss your objection

If an LPA has been obtained you can have grounds for revoking an LPA

Under section 22(3) of the Mental Capacity Act 2005, the Court of Protection may revoke a LPA if it is satisfied that:

- fraud or undue pressure was used to induce the Donor to create the LPA; or
- the attorney of the LPA:
    - has behaved, or is behaving, in a way that contravenes his authority or is not in the Donor's best interests; or

- proposes to behave in a way that would contravene his authority or would not be in the Donor's best interests.

Revoking an LPA is serious step and the Court of Protection will look at all the circumstances, including the level of the offending or prospective behaviours.

The Court will also consider whether it is necessary and proportionate to revoke an LPA and ultimately, whether the revocation would be in the Donor's best interests. The following cases show the approach taken by the Court of Protection in making a decision on revocation.

Deputies

Contacting the OPG

Where a person lacks capacity ("P"), the Court of Protection has the power to appoint a person to make decisions on their behalf. This person is known as a deputy.

A deputy is usually given a variety of powers by the Court of Protection in relation to the property and affairs, including the control, management, acquisition, and disposition of property of the person who lacks capacity.

A deputy may have the power to carry on any profession, trade or business on behalf of the person who lacks capacity; this may include discharging their debts and obligations and conducting legal proceedings in their name. The scope of the deputy's authority will be set out in the Deputyship Order.

The Court of Protection also has the power to remove a deputy in accordance with section 16(8) of the Mental Capacity Act 2005.

Overall the Court may suspend or discharge the appointment of a deputy if it is satisfied that the deputy: has behaved, or is behaving, in a way that contravenes the authority conferred on him by the Court or is not in P's best interests; or proposes to behave in a way that contravenes the authority conferred on him by the Court or is not in P's best interests.

If a deputy acts outside the scope of his or her powers and/or is misappropriating and mismanaging property of the person who lacks capacity, it is possible to seek their replacement.

The Court will consider whether it is in the best interests of the person who lacks capacity to have the deputy removed and replaced.

As the case of Re CJ [2015] reveals deputies can be removed.

The Judge held that although there was no dishonest misappropriation of CJ's (person who lacked capacity) funds, MP (the deputy) had failed to comply and co-operate with the Court of Protection and the Office of the Public Guardian.

The Deputy had failed to keep all financial records and submit a report to the Office of the Public Guardian as and when required. To turn a blind eye to MP's refusal to comply with his duties would undermine the safeguarding work carried out by the Office of the Public Guardian.

The Judge was satisfied that MP (the deputy) had behaved in a way that contravened the authority given to him and confirmed that MP ought to be removed as CJ's (person who lacked capacity) deputy.

TIP

At the LPA level your ability to revoke/rein in the powers of the Attorney/Deputy are dependent on your ability to influence the Office of Public Guardian and/or Court of Protection. Your options are limited, and you may be more likely to achieve justice once the person has died though the OPG will not investigate once someone has died.

However, it is a sad state of affairs that unless you have a compelling case the police and authorities are unlikely to get involved. As a consequence, the role of the lawyer is going to be important.

After Death – What are the variables which indicate LPA/probate fraud?

Factors to look out for:

- Have there been changes to the will particularly if the deceased changed their will soon before they died, naming new beneficiaries, or including people that the family aren't familiar with?
- Did the deceased seek legal advice in making the new will, or create a homemade or online will?
- Could the deceased have been unduly influenced or coerced into changing their will, or have no knowledge that their will has been changed?
- Have certain family members been frozen out?
- Could the will have been forged?
- Did the deceased's deputy seek to make a statutory will?
- Have there been changes in the deceased's financial behaviour before or after death
- Any unusual or unaccountable cash withdrawals or transfers made from the deceased's bank accounts prior to, or soon after, death.
- Was another person being added to their bank account prior to death?
- Was an 'unexpected' attorney appointed prior to death?
- Have personal items been removed from the home of the deceased, or are they unaccounted for?

What Are The Attributes of Someone Who Commits LPA & Probate Fraud?

The sad reality is that most probate and LPA fraud is not detected

There are many attributes which those executors or attorneys display which enable them to conduct criminal behaviour and be confident that they can get away with it including:

- They Exercise Strong Influence on the Vulnerable Person – The key thing that a would-be probate/LPA fraudster (Lets call him or her, X) will do is to exercise influence and manoeuvre the vulnerable person to give sole control (or effective control) of his or her assets to X. At a practical level, this can involve X becoming sole attorney and effective sole executor (or the other attorneys/executors are manoeuvred away), X changing the will (they apply undue influence but typically try to get the vulnerable to see a lawyer) of the vulnerable person and taking assets out of the estate either before and/or after death.

- They Are Ruthless – To cut to the chase in my experience, the person X is utterly self-serving and cold blooded. Typically, other relatives (would be beneficiaries)) under-estimate the lengths that X will go to get what he or she wants. This puts X at a fundamental advantage as they use any card possible to achieve their objectives.

- They Are Convincing – From my knowledge, X will try to be convincing and will have no hesitation in lying, manipulating, or accounting for his or her actions. I have seen would be LPA/fraudsters have no problem about lying (convincingly) about what is in the estate, why they have ignored judicial orders and will come up with a variety of delaying tactics for sapping the morale of other beneficiaries.

- They Have Excellent Knowledge of the Law –The successful individuals who get away with probate/LPA fraud have a good understanding of the law and will act accordingly. Typically, X will understand that while acting as an attorney it is difficult for other family members to show wrongdoing as they do not have access to the bank accounts which is a key piece of evidence Also, X knows that the Office of the Public Guardian will not investigate once the person dies which gives practical powerful legal protection. If X is appointed sole executor the legal rights of the proper beneficiaries can be limited and if so, X will exploit this.

- They Minimise Their Tracks – Probably the biggest Achilles-heel of a potential LPA/Probate fraudster is the lack of ability to cover their tracks. What can cause his or her undoing is simple greed and/or lack of patience. Thus, the successful LPA & Probate fraudster will be very careful in the way in which they take money out of the estate otherwise they run the risk of getting caught.

Often it turns out that the executor is the same person as the person who was appointed as Attorney. If not, you can pressurise the executor to seek recourse against the errant attorney by reminding him or her of the oath.

Executors

From experience the majority of fraud cases involving executors have also been individuals who have had control of the Deceased's affairs prior to death and often were attorney and exercised influence in the creation of a will.

The content of the oath sworn by personal representatives reflects the statutory duties of the personal representatives (Section 25, AEA 1925):

- *Collect and get in the real and personal estate of the deceased and administer it according to law.*

- *When required to do so by the court, exhibit on oath in the court a full inventory of the estate and when so required render an account of the administration of the estate to the court.*

- *When required to do so by the High Court, deliver up the grant of probate or administration to that court.*

The key way to attack an errant executor is to obtain information and then use that information in a clever way which puts your client in a better position.

It may be worth reminding the executor of their legal duty and their oath if they made one?

At a practical level, you can seek to pressurise the executor/LPA to produce an inventory and account. (Please see Chapter 3)

Disclosure

TIP

Nearly every case of LPA and Executor fraud case I deal with (apart from Will fraud) focuses on bank statements. This is often so key. If you can get hold of the bank statements it really can make such a difference.

Disclosure of Documents – You can refer to the Actaps Code.

http://www.actaps.com/draft.cfm

> *2.4 The aim of the early disclosure of documents by the defendant is not to encourage "fishing expeditions" by the claimant, but to promote an early exchange of relevant information to help in clarifying or resolving issues in dispute.*
>
> *The claimant's solicitors can assist by identifying in the letter of claim or in a subsequent letter the particular documents or categories of documents which they consider are relevant, and by providing copies of these where appropriate.*
>
> *2.5 All documents are disclosed on the basis that they are not to be disclosed to third parties (other than legal advisers) or used for any purpose other than the resolution of the dispute, unless otherwise agreed in writing or permitted by the court.*
>
> *Objectives of pre-action conduct and protocols*

3. Before commencing proceedings, the court will expect the parties to have exchanged sufficient information to—

(a) understand each other's position;

(b) make decisions about how to proceed;

(c) try to settle the issues without proceedings;

(d) consider a form of Alternative Dispute Resolution (ADR) to assist with settlement.

(e) support the efficient management of those proceedings; and

(f) reduce the costs of resolving the dispute.

Proportionality

4. A pre-action protocol or this Practice Direction must not be used by a party as a tactical device to secure an unfair advantage over another party. Only reasonable and proportionate steps should be taken by the parties to identify, narrow, and resolve the legal, factual or expert issues.

5. The costs incurred in complying with a pre-action protocol or this Practice Direction should be proportionate (CPR 44.3(5)). Where parties incur disproportionate costs in complying with any pre-action protocol or this Practice Direction, those costs will not be recoverable as part of the costs of the proceedings.

Steps before issuing a claim at court

6. Where there is a relevant pre-action protocol, the parties should comply with that protocol before commencing proceedings. Where there is no relevant pre-action protocol, the parties should exchange correspondence and information to comply with the objectives in paragraph 3, bearing in mind that compliance should be proportionate. The steps will usually include—

(a) the claimant writing to the defendant with concise details of the claim. The letter should include the basis on which the claim is made,

a summary of the facts, what the claimant wants from the defendant, and if money, how the amount is calculated.

(b) the defendant responding within a reasonable time – 14 days in a straight forward case and no more than 3 months in a very complex one. The reply should include confirmation as to whether the claim is accepted and, if it is not accepted, the reasons why, together with an explanation as to which facts and parts of the claim are disputed and whether the defendant is making a counterclaim as well as providing details of any counterclaim; and

(c) the parties disclosing key documents relevant to the issues in dispute.

Linked with this, consider Making Pre-Action applications for Disclosure but this must be a last resort due to the costs risks [46] If I am to make some kind of Court application, I like to use Part 64 proceedings which we have covered elsewhere. [47]

The starting point is Civil Procedure Rule 31.16. This sets out the four-stage test that must be satisfied for the court to make an order. It reads:

(1) 'This rule applies when an application is made to the court under any act for disclosure before proceedings have started.

(2) The application must be supported by evidence.

(3) The court may make an order under this rule only where:

(a) The party is likely to be a party to subsequent proceedings.

(b) The applicant is also likely to be a party to those proceedings.

(c) If proceedings are started, the respondent's duty by way of standard disclosure, set out in rule 31.6, would extend to the documents or classes of documents of which the applicant seeks disclosure.

---

[46] I would need some very good evidence to make such an application due to the cost's risks- https://www.lawgazette.co.uk/practice-points/pre-action-disc

[47] https://www.justice.gov.uk/courts/procedure-rules/civil/rules/part64

(d) Disclosure before proceedings have started is desirable in order to:

i. Dispose fairly of the anticipated proceedings.

ii. Assist the dispute to be resolved without proceedings.

iii. Save costs.'

You will be expected to demonstrate that:

- the respondent is likely to be a party to subsequent proceedings.
- the document(s) would be disclosable as part of standard disclosure if proceedings were issued (in effect, that they are relevant to the potential claim); and
- early disclosure is desirable in order to dispose fairly of the proceedings, to assist the dispute to be resolved without proceedings, or to save costs.

A potential claimant does not have to establish the merits of their claim, but the court has discretion to decide whether, given all the facts of the case, disclosure of the documents sought should be granted.

The court will also expect to see evidence that you have set out your potential claim in a letter before action, and sought voluntary disclosure, before applying to the court for assistance.[48]

TIP

The sad reality is that if you are dealing with some kind of probate and LPA fraud the other side (and their lawyers) are not going to disclose documents even if they should in accordance with Pre-Action Protocols and the CPR generally or Actaps Code. Thus, you are looking at some form of targeted legal application.

[48] closure-not-worth-the-candle/5062147.article

In addition, when I am faced with cases of possible LPA and/or Executor fraud one of the things which I will often is to instruct a forensic accountant to do an analysis. It is much more difficult for an opponent (or their legal team) to dismiss your client's position if you have someone more independent and credible objecting.

What is 'fraud' when disputing a will?

If you are faced with the dramatic situation where you may be alleging in the context of will making, 'fraud' this is a wide definition and encompasses various scenarios. If the true intentions of the testator are not contained within their will, it could be argued that a fraud has occurred.

Examples of fraud in the context of wills include:

- impersonation of the testator by a fraudster to execute the will
- misleading the testator to sign a will when they believe the document to be another document
- a beneficiary making false representations to the testator about the character of a potential other beneficiary to deceive the testator to leave more monies to the perpetrator of the false representation
- the destruction of the testator's will with the intention of gaining from the estate as a result of the rules of intestacy

Usually, the instruction of a specialist handwriting expert will be required to obtain a report as to whether, in their professional opinion, the will and/or the signature is that of the testator's. However, the court still must consider all evidence and a handwriting expert's opinion will not always be conclusive.

Forgery

As a general proposition, the Courts are reluctant to find that a forgery has occurred and will require a higher degree of proof than usual when making such a finding.

If the evidence of a handwriting expert is obtained which indicates fraud it is unlikely to be the final word. Indeed, there are cases where, despite fairly strong confirmation from handwriting experts that there is "very positive evidence" of forgery, the Courts have not found one to have occurred (see for instance Fuller v Strum [2002] 1 WLR 1097 although later subject to appeal the trial Judges preference for the evidence of the lay witnesses over that of the handwriting expert was not overturned).

In addition to the evidence regarding the signature, the Court may take into account other factors when determining whether the document is a forgery (if this is alleged). There are a number of factors in this case which may be relied on to support any assertion that a is forged and which the Court may regard as relevant, including:

a) The form of the document

b) The time frame of the document.

c) The choice of witnesses to the will which may raise concerns given the independent witnesses previously employed by the alleged testator.

d) Whether the two witnesses to the alleged Will can give evidence.

e) The circumstances surrounding the discovery of the Later will

How can you contest a will on the grounds of undue influence, fraud or forgery?[49]

[49] An interesting article appears here :https://www.thegazette.co.uk/all-notices/content/101098

Undue Influence

When a claim of undue influence is made, the burden of proof shifts to the person alleging the undue influence. However, recent case law has seen the courts more willing to accept arguments that undue influence has taken place. A good example is the case of Schrader v Schrader [2013][50], involving a mother who left her home in its entirety to her son Nick. The Court took the mother's vulnerability, her dependence on her son Nick, the engagement of a will-writer at Nick's behest with no prior contact with the family, and Nick's character and violent history into account when reaching their decision which was that undue influence had taken place. Her Will was therefore found to be invalid, and her estate passed under the terms of a previous Will she had made.

Practical Problems

Proving fraud, forgery or undue influence in court is difficult. The burden of proof for these three claims is evidential threshold is high and usually, by their very nature, these sorts of events tend to happen in secret and therefore actually finding any evidence of it happening to get over this burden can be tricky.

An alternative claim for disappointed claimants who have these sorts of concerns is to raise an allegation that the testator did not have knowledge and approval of the will. If this is pleaded, once suspicious circumstances are established (of the kind outlined above) the lower burden of proof of 'on the balance of probabilities' applies and the onus is shifted to the propounder of the will to establish its validity.

If you believe the deceased person lacked the mental capacity to make a valid Will or was unduly influenced or coerced into making or changing a Will, there is no specific time limit to contest the Will.

If you believe a Will was incorrectly executed in accordance with the legal formalities for making a Will. There is, again, no specific time limit to contest the Will.

---

[50] https://www.casemine.com/judgement/uk/5a8ff74160d03e7f57eaa7b5

If you believe a Will is fraudulent and has been forged, there is no time limit for contesting the Will.

TIP

When I am faced with these kinds of cases I spend a lot of time trying to honestly think what has happened and to consider how this will play out in the witness box.

CHAPTER NINE

MEDIATION – INTRODUCTION AND LAW

What is Mediation and How Does It Contrast to Other Forms of Dispute Resolution?

Mediation is shuttle diplomacy, or mediated communication.

The essence of shuttle diplomacy is the use of a third party to convey information back and forth between the parties, serving as a reliable means of communication less susceptible to the grandstanding of face-to-face or media-based communication.

The intermediary serves not only as a relay for questions and answers, but can also provide suggestions for moving the conflict toward resolution and does so in private.

There is no specific set format for mediation but many mediators will follow a format of having an opening session and then holding private sessions with the parties.

This is where the parties select an independent third party or neutral to assist the parties in reaching an acceptable solution. The mediator will discuss the problems with the parties both together and separately in private sessions known as "caucuses."

As we see below it generally follows the format of going back and forth between the parties.

The uses of mediation

Mediation can be used in a variety of circumstances such as:

- Family Disputes.

- Inheritance Disputes.
- Trusts.
- Tax.
- International Business Relationships.

Why mediation works

There are many reasons that mediation often works well. These include:

- Focus – Commercial mediation has a pressure chamber to concentrate the mind in a way that can only be otherwise done by more formal legal proceedings. The parties are more likely to be committed to the process where they require outside assistance.
- Neutrality – A mediator can bring freshness and flexibility to problem solving; apply more leverage to encourage movement in the parties. It is possible for the mediator to win respect from the parties.
- Confidences – The ability of the Mediator to secure confidences means that the mediator can understand what is important to the parties.
- Taking heat out of the proceedings – Often a mediator can allow the parties to give vent to their anger but allow them to make a point ad soften the blow. One party may say to the mediator in private session "X lied to me about this." The mediator can say to X – "Y thinks differently about this. What do you say?"
- Focusing on Solutions – A mediator can help be a catalyst for parties to focus on solutions which a Court or a Tribunal cannot order.

It plays a role within elderly client issues as it can represent a fast-track way of settling cases without the need to go to Court.

How does it contrast to other forms of Alternative Dispute Resolution?

Negotiation

Settling disputes by direct negotiation of the parties is the commonest way that disputes are settled. It is only when direct negotiation breaks down that some other means of settlement is required. Negotiation is the starting point for any form of dispute resolution

Arbitration

The core process of arbitration is the process of investigation and judgment by a third party. This has mimicked lawyer litigation habits of formalism and being adversarial. Its core purpose is resolution by external investigation and judgment.

Conciliation

This is a loosely defined word. More often it uses a process at which the conciliator produces a recommendation as to how the dispute should be settled if it not possible for the parties to reach an agreement. It is well known in employment law circles due to the involvement of ACAS in the assistance of resolution of disputes.

Expert Evaluation

As a preliminary step to settlement the parties sometimes agree to engage an expert to investigate and report on the dispute. They may also agree to abide the opinion of the Expert. This is often classified as an ADR process but is more like litigation or arbitration in that it leads to a binding (and typically non-appealable) decision.

Mediation/Arbitration

The Mediator is asked to provide a recommendation on how the dispute should be settled, which if not be accepted may be referred to arbitration. This is underutilised and can be an effective way of resolving disputes.

Early Neutral Evaluation

The parties appoint a neutral third party (often a retired Judge) to make a preliminary assessment of the facts or legal merits of the dispute. The neutral will give a non-binding evaluation of the prospects of success.

This is an overlooked provision of the CPR is rule 3.1(2)(m) which provides that the court may 'take any other step or make any other order for the purpose of managing the case and furthering the overriding objective, including hearing an early neutral evaluation with the aim of helping the parties settle the case'.

Whereas mediation is not concerned with considering the merits of a matter, this lies at the very core of ENE. ENE is therefore potentially of huge value in disputes where parties have vastly opposing stances and, perhaps, where one party may be oblivious of the realities of the case in hand (for example, where their claim is hopeless and/or they do not understand the risks of litigation).[51]

TIP

Always be open to cases settling (even those which appear entrenched). I was dealing with a bitter case at court and the words of our barrister with the opposing one enabled a partial settlement which significantly narrowed the issues.

What Is the Law of Mediation?

UK legislation & case law

The Courts and case law underpin mediation.

With respect to the "overriding objective" of the CPR is to enable courts to deal with the parties justly.

[51] In the Court of Appeal case Lomax v Lomax [2019 EWCA Civ 1467). the court concluded that there was no reason to imply into CPR 3.1(2)(m) any limitation on the courts' power to order an ENE hearing so that the consent of the parties is required. Such an interpretation, the court explained, 'would be inconsistent with elements of the overriding objective, in particular the saving of expense and allotting to cases an appropriate share of the court's resources, and would, therefore, be contrary to rule 1.2(b)'. The decision in Lomax is a significant development on the issue of ADR compulsion within the civil court process.

The requirement for consideration of ADR prior to the issue of proceedings in relation to all types of cases including elderly client issues.

8. Litigation should be a last resort. As part of a relevant pre-action protocol or this Practice Direction, the parties should consider whether negotiation or some other form of ADR might enable them to settle their dispute without commencing proceedings.

9. Parties should continue to consider the possibility of reaching a settlement at all times, including after proceedings have been started. Part 36 offers may be made before proceedings are issued.

10. Parties may negotiate to settle a dispute or may use a form of ADR including—

(a) mediation, a third party facilitating a resolution;

(b) arbitration, a third party deciding the dispute;

(c) early neutral evaluation, a third party giving an informed opinion on the dispute; and

The Court of Appeal has ruled in Halsey[52] "*All members of the legal profession who conduct litigation should now routinely consider with their clients whether their disputes are suitable for ADR.*"

The Civil Procedure Rules

- Part 1 – the overriding objective – the court has a duty to encourage the parties to use an ADR procedure if appropriate and to facilitate the use of such a procedure.

  Rule 1.4(2) sets out the activities the court may undertake which constitute active case management. These include:

(e) encouraging the parties to use an alternative dispute resolution procedure if the court considers that appropriate and facilitating use of such procedure;

---

[52] Halsey v Milton Keynes General NHS Trust 2004 EWCA Civ 303

(f) helping parties to settle the whole or part of the case."

- Part 3 & 26 – The court's case management powers include the ability to stay the proceedings for a certain period to allow ADR.

  CPR Rule 26.4(1) provides that the court may "stay" proceedings where a party makes "*a written request for the proceedings to be stayed while the parties try to settle the case by alternative dispute resolution or other means" when filing the allocation questionnaire."*

- After statements of case have been filed (the allocation stage) the parties can request a one month stay to attempt to settle the claim through negotiation or ADR.

- The practice direction on pre-action protocols provides that parties should, prior to issuing proceedings, consider whether some form of ADR procedure will be more suitable than litigation and should provide evidence that ADR was considered. There are also pre-action protocols for specific types of dispute (e.g. professional negligence, construction disputes and so on) that provide for the parties actively to consider ADR.

  > *The Practice Direction to CPR Part 26 also states, at para 12.2, that where the court has ordered an amount of money to be paid by one party to another, the court give directions that may include "staying the claim while the parties try to settle the case by alternative dispute resolution or other means."*

- The costs rules (part 44.3) provide that the conduct of the parties before, as well as during, proceedings will be taken into account when making a costs award including the extent to which parties followed any relevant pre-action protocols and the efforts they made to try to resolve the dispute. This allows the court to penalise in costs a party who has refused to participate in ADR even if the party subsequently succeeds at trial.

- There are also a number of different court guides which set out the approach of that particular court in encouraging ADR. For example, the Commercial Court (a court in London which deals with high value business disputes) has devised an order directing the parties to attempt ADR. Many courts have now launched their own mediation schemes though there is nothing specific within the elderly client sphere.

Case Law

The new rules generated interest but there was still no radical change in litigation practice notwithstanding the clear duty on solicitors to consider ADR. However the Court of Appeal) began handing down a series of decisions in which they emphasised the requirements of the new regime.

In Muman v Nagasena[53] the Court of Appeal made one of the first examples of an order on its initiative to stay court proceedings to allow ADR. Lord Justice Mummery stated:

> "*It is time for mediation. No more money should be spent from the assets of this charity.....until all efforts have been made to secure a mediation of this dispute.*"

In Cowl v Plymouth City Council[54] the Court of Appeal stated that in disputes between public bodies and members of the public, the parties should be acutely conscious of the contribution ADR can make to resolving disputes in a manner which meets the needs of the parties and saves time, expense and stress. Lord Woolf, giving the leading judgement, stated:

> "*This case will have served some purpose if it makes clear that the lawyers acting on both sides of a dispute of this sort are under a heavy obligation to resort to litigation only if it is really unavoidable.*"

However the decision which is generally viewed as the "high watermark" in encouraging ADR was given by the Court of Appeal in *Dunnett v Railtrack* in 2002[55].

---

[53] Muman v Nagasena 1999 EWCA Civ 764

[54] Cowl v Plymouth City Council 1 WLR 803 2002

[55] Dunnett v Railtrack 2002 EWCA Civ 302 2002 1 WLR 2434

The facts of the case were that Mrs Dunnett owned some horses which grazed on land next to a railway line which Railtrack was responsible for. Railtrack was under a statutory duty to have gated access to the line which could not be locked. Trespassers left the gate open and three of Mrs Dunnett's horses were hit by a train and killed. Mrs Dunnett, acting as a litigant in person, sued Railtrack. Mrs Dunnett lost her claim at first instance but obtained leave to appeal to the Court of Appeal. At the permission stage, the Court of Appeal suggested the parties try to mediate but Railtrack refused. It argued that it would probably have to bear the costs of any mediation (Mrs Dunnett was impecunious) and that it would necessarily involve Railtrack paying Mrs Dunnett some compensation to dispose of the claim which it was not prepared to do given that it considered (rightly as it turned out) that it had a very strong claim. Railtrack proceeded with, and won, its appeal (as it had predicted) and therefore it expected costs to be awarded in its favour. However, the Court of Appeal refused to award Railtrack its costs of the appeal.

Brooke LJ stated:

> "*When asked by the court why [Railtrack] were not willing to contemplate alternative dispute resolution, [Railtrack] said that this would necessarily involve the payment of money, which [Railtrack] were not willing to contemplate, over and above what they had already offered. This appears to be a misunderstanding of the purpose of alternative dispute resolution. Skilled mediators are now able to achieve results satisfactory to both parties in many cases which are quite beyond the power of lawyers and courts to achieve. This court has knowledge of cases were intense feelings have arisen, for instance in relation to clinical negligence claims. But when the parties are brought together on neutral soil with a skilled mediator to help them resolve their differences, it may very well be that the mediator is able to achieve a result by which the parties shake hands at the end and feel that they have gone away having settled the dispute on terms with which they are happy to live. A mediator may be able to provide solutions which are beyond the powers of the court to provide. Occasions are known to the court in claims against the police, which can give rise to as much passion as a claim of this kind where a claimant's precious horses are killed on a railway line, by which an apology from a very senior police officer is all that the claimant is really seeking and the money side of the matter*

falls away.

It is to be hoped that any publicity given to this part of the judgment.....will draw the attention of lawyers to their duties to further the overriding objective.....and to the possibility that, if they turn down out of hand the chance of [ADR] when suggested by the court, as happened on this occasion, they may have to face uncomfortable costs consequence".

Dunnett was therefore the first example of the court using its costs sanctions to punish a party who refused to pursue ADR and accordingly was very significant.

For example it was applied in:

Neal v Jones Motors[56] where a successful party's recoverable costs were reduced by £5,000 for failure to follow Court's recommendations to mediate.

Royal Bank of Canada v Secretary of State for Defence[57]- The judge held that a willingness to mediate was something which was significant in deciding where costs were to lie. Accordingly he made no order as to costs, thus penalising the winning department.

Virani v Manuel Revert Y CIA SA[58] The Court of Appeal was forced to decide in what currency the claimant's damages were to be awarded. On the application for permission to appeal, the defendant appellant had been offered the Court of Appeal's mediation service offered by the single Lord Justice. Notwithstanding such offer, the appellant declined to enter into any form of mediation. The refusal led to the penalty of the successful respondent's costs being assessed on the indemnity, as supposed to the standard basis of assessment.

Courts have jurisdiction to impose a costs sanction on successful parties who unreasonably decline to mediate. In deciding whether or not to do

---

[56] Neal v Jones Motors 2002 EWCA 1730

[57] Royal Bank of Canada v Secretary of State for Defence 2003 EWHC 1841

[58] Virani v Manuel Revert Y CIA SA 2003

so, factors to consider include whether the successful party reasonably believed they would win, cost benefit, and whether the unsuccessful party can show that mediation had a reasonable prospect of success. There is a considerable risk of a costs sanction where a judge's recommendation to mediate is ignored.

On 11 May 2004, the Court of Appeal handed down its judgment in the conjoined appeals of *Halsey v Milton Keynes NHS Trust and Steel v Joy and Halliday.* The court was given the opportunity to look at when it might order costs against a successful party who refused to mediate at the invitation of the unsuccessful party. In Halsey, a clinical negligence claim, the claimant's solicitors repeatedly invited mediation of the defendant Trust, which repeatedly declined because it correctly predicted that they were not liable on what was anyway a low quantum claim. The judge declined to deprive the Trust of its costs on winning, finding 'somewhat tactical' motives on the claimant solicitor's part, who was funding the case on CFA with a 100 per cent success fee. The appeal was limited to the issue of that costs order.

In reaching its decision the court articulated the following principles:

- To oblige truly unwilling parties to refer their disputes to mediation would be to impose an unacceptable obstruction on their right of access to the courts.

- In deciding whether to deprive a successful party of all or some of its costs for refusing to go to ADR it had to be borne in mind that this was an exception to the general rule in CPR Part 44.3(2) and the burden was on the unsuccessful party to show why the general rule should be departed from.

- Such a departure was not justified unless it could be shown that the successful litigant acted unreasonably having regard to all the circumstances of the case.

However the court considered the following as important but non-exhaustive factors to be taken into account:

- The nature of the dispute: some matters were intrinsically unsuitable for ADR.

- The merits of the case: a party's reasonable belief that he had a strong case would be relevant to reasonableness of his refusal of ADR, for otherwise the fears of costs sanctions might be used to extract unmerited settlements.

- Whether other settlement methods had been attempted but rejected.

- Whether the costs of the mediation would be disproportionately high.

- Delay: this might be relevant if mediation was suggested late in the day and the effect of accepting it at that stage would be to delay the trial.

- Whether the mediation had a reasonable prospect of success.

- Whether the court had encouraged mediation: the more that the court had encouraged mediation, the more likely it was that the unsuccessful party would discharge the burden showing the successful party's refusal was unreasonable.

Two important points arise from *National Westminster Bank Plc v Thomas Feeney* and *Linda Feeney* [2006] EWHC 90066 (Costs) and [2007] (Costs Appeal).

First, Eady J confirmed that as a matter of general principle, costs incurred in a mediation would form part of the costs of the action just as any reasonable costs of negotiation would (see Costs Practice Direction para.4.6(8)).

Secondly, the successful party did not recover the mediator's costs or its costs for preparing for and attending at the mediation because: (a) the mediation agreement entered in to by the parties on the mediation providers standard terms was on the basis that the mediators fee would be borne equally by the parties who would bear their own costs; (b) the Tomlin Order agreed when settlement was reached did not deal explicitly with the costs of the mediation and (c) it was held that the Tomlin Order did not alter the mediation agreement.

In Lobster Group Ltd v Heidelberg Graphic Equipment Ltd [2008] EWHC 413 (TCC) Coulson J, having confirmed the main point in Feeney (that a Tomlin Order will not alter a mediation agreement unless it does so explicitly) went on to make finding that has significant implications for mediation costs. He introduced some doubt about whether the costs of a mediation would (assuming no contractual agreement of the type in Feeney) form part of the costs of the action in cases where a mediation takes place pre-proceedings.

Post-Halsey case law: When is it unreasonable to refuse to mediate?

Parties cannot be compelled to use an Alternative Dispute Resolution (ADR) procedure such as mediation to resolve their disputes. Yet, for around two decades now, a pro-ADR approach has become an integral part of our litigation culture in the UK, with pre-action protocols, the Civil Procedure Rules and the Jackson reforms all promoting the use of ADR whenever appropriate. Endorsing this culture, the courts have encouraged parties to use ADR, particularly mediation, and they have imposed costs sanctions where they consider parties have unreasonably refused to engage in the process.

In Burchell v Bullard & Others [2005] EWCA Civ 358 the court considered that the nature of the case (a small building dispute) lent itself to mediation; and the cost of mediating was small ("a drop in the ocean" the court said) when compared to the cost of litigation in a case of this kind.

In Garritt-Critchley and others v Ronnan and another [2014] EWHC 1774 (Ch), the defendants were ordered to pay the claimant's costs on an indemnity basis because their position of consistently refusing to mediate due to confidence in their position and a belief that the parties were too far apart, was wrong.

In 2017, the Court of Appeal heard two appeals on the reasonableness of a party's refusal to engage in mediation, with very contrasting outcomes. In Thakkar v Patel, the Court held that to remain silent in the face of an offer to mediate is, absent exceptional circumstances, unreasonable conduct that merits a costs sanction. In Gore v Naheed , the Court refused to penalise the claimant in costs for his failure to engage with the defendant's proposal to mediate.

It is difficult to reconcile these two Court of Appeal judgments. Thakker follows the harder line of authorities where the courts have encouraged mediation and imposed costs sanctions on those who refuse to engage, drag their feet in the process or remain silent when invited to participate in mediation. Gore took a softer approach where a party can reasonably refuse mediation if the legal issues are complex or if he/she has doubts over whether a mediation would successfully resolve the dispute.

In DSN v Blackpool Football Club Ltd [2020] EWHC 670 (QB) (20 March 2020), the judge considered that indemnity costs should apply because of the defendant's refusal to engage in mediation. This was conduct "out of the norm" as the court did not accept the defendant's justification that it believed it had a strong defence. No defence by itself justified a failure to engage in any kind of ADR.

The Without Prejudice rule – How Confidential are Your Mediations and Settlement Meetings?[59]

Parties have long been encouraged, as a matter of public policy, to discuss settlement privately with a view to avoiding trial:

> "*communications made with a view to an amicable settlement ought to be held very sacred; for if parties were to be afterwards prejudiced by their efforts to compromise, it would be impossible to attempt an amicable arrangement of differences.*"[60]

In the context of mediation Dyson LJ said, in *Halsey v Milton Keynes*

[59] There is excellent consideration of this issue by the leading mediator, Tim Wallis in PIBULJ July 2009

[60] Romilly M.R. in Hoghton v Hoghton (1852) 15 Beav 278, 321)

General NHS Trust[61]

> "... *parties are entitled in an ADR to adopt whatever position they wish and if, thus the dispute is not settled, that is not a matter for the court... if the integrity and confidentiality of the process is to be respected, the court should not know, and therefore should not investigate, why the process did not result in agreement.*"

Integral to the success of mediation is the concept of confidentiality: parties are encouraged to negotiate openly and realistically, unfettered by concerns that what they disclose in the process might be used against them in the future, in legal proceedings or otherwise. Provided at common law, and typically reinforced by a mediation agreement to which the parties sign up, this protection is seen as sacrosanct by mediators and clients alike.

However, a recent decision in the High Court shows us it is not unqualified.

In Berkeley Square Holdings & Ors v Lancer Property Asset Management Ltd & Ors [2020] EWHC 1015 (Ch) the judge explored the exceptions to the without prejudice rule. He went on to set out a useful summary of the position, indicating that privilege that would otherwise protect negotiations may in principle be set aside in the following situations:

(a) where there is a dispute over whether the negotiations have resulted in a concluded settlement;

(b) where one party claims that the negotiated settlement should be set aside because of fraud, misrepresentation or undue influence;

(c) where, despite the absence of a settlement, an estoppel is said to arise out of something said during negotiations;

(d) where privilege is being used as a cloak for perjury, blackmail or

---

[61] [2004] EWCA Civ 576; [2004] 1 W.L.R. 3002 (at paragraph 14)

other 'unambiguous impropriety';

(e) where evidence of the negotiations could be used explain delay or apparent acquiescence;

(f) where it be relevant to the interpretation of the settlement agreement to admit objective facts referred to in the negotiations;

(g) where the notoriously difficult 'Muller exception' circumstances arise – seemingly where (i) there is no issue as to the truth or falsity of anything stated in the negotiations; and (ii) admitting evidence of what was said is necessary in order to ensure that an issue raised by one party is 'fairly justiciable'; and (iii) there is no adverse effect on the protection to which the other parties are entitled.

In this case, the Judge held that two of those exceptions applied: (b) – fraud, and (g) – Muller.

As to the former, he rejected the Claimants' case that the exception existed to protect only the victim of fraud, and that the Defendants should not be allowed to 'turn the rule on its head'. If privileged evidence of negotiations may be introduced to prove that a settlement should be set aside due to fraud, he said, then it is equally legitimate to do so in response to an allegation of fraud.

Here the Defendants were permitted to introduce the contentious passages from their mediation position statement, and the matter proceeded to trial. Meanwhile, the wider significance of the judgment (putting aside the minor extension to the scope of the fraud exception) is to offer the most comprehensive and up to date analysis of the law in this area. Importantly, it acts as a useful reminder to practitioners and their clients that what is said in a mediation will not, in absolutely every case, remain within the four walls of the room in which it is disclosed – whether made of bricks and mortar, or something more virtual.

What are the Key Elderly Client Issues?

Beyond focusing on the CPR and the relevant case referred to above there are specific legislation relevant to within the elderly client sphere:

TIP

When trying to persuade a party to mediate initially refer them to the CPR rules and focus on the benefits of mediation. Be relentless – If they keep resisting keep pressing and add some threat into what you are doing. I once dealt with a case where the other party persistently ignored and evaded my offer of mediation. Towards the end of this sequence of correspondence I was writing "My client has offered to mediate on eight occasions." Eventually they agreed to mediate.

MCA Code of Practice

The Code of Practice to the Mental Capacity Act (MCA) 2005 provides guidance to decision makers about managing "conflicting concerns" when establishing the best interests of a person who lacks capacity.

> *5.64 The decision-maker will need to find a way of balancing these concerns or deciding between them. The first approach should be to review all elements of the best interests checklist with everyone involved. They should include the person who lacks capacity (as much as they are able to take part) and anyone who has been involved in earlier discussions. It may be possible to reach an agreement at a meeting to air everyone's concerns. But an agreement in itself might not be in the person's best interests. Ultimate responsibility for working out best interests lies with the decision-maker.*
>
> *15.7 A mediator helps people to come to an agreement that is acceptable to all parties. Mediation can help solve a problem at an early stage. It offers a wider range of solutions than the court can – and it may be less stressful for all parties, more cost-effective and quicker. People who come to an agreement through mediation are more likely to keep to it, because they have taken part in decision-making.*
>
> *15.8 Mediators are independent. They have no personal interest in the*

outcome of a case. They do not make decisions or impose solutions. The mediator will decide whether the case is suitable for mediation. They will consider the likely chances of success and the need to protect the interests of the person who lacks capacity.

15.9 Any case that can be settled through negotiation is likely to benefit from mediation. It is most suitable when people are not communicating well or not understanding each other's point of view. It can improve relationships and stop future disputes, so it is a good option when it is in the person's interests for people to have a good relationship in the future.

15.10 In mediation, everybody needs to take part as equally as possible so that a mediator can help everyone involved to focus on the person's best interests. It might also be appropriate to involve an advocate to help communicate the wishes of the person who lacks capacity.

15.11 The National Mediation Helpline helps callers to identify an effective means of resolving their difficulty without going to court. It will arrange an appointment with a trained and accredited mediator.

15.12 Healthcare and social care staff may also take part in mediation processes. But it may be more appropriate to follow the relevant healthcare or social care complaints procedures (see paragraphs 15.14-32)

15.13 In certain situations (mainly family mediation), legal aid may be available to fund mediation for people who meet the qualifying criteria (see paragraphs 15.38–15.44).

Trusts

In the case of hostile trusts disputes where trustees find themselves caught in the crossfire between the demands of the competing beneficiaries, costs protection may be sought from the Court by way of an application under CPR 64.2 (a) for an order authorising a neutral position to be adopted. As long as a neutral stance is subsequently taken the trustee should avoid personal exposure. However, pitfalls remain and neutrality in practice is not always an easy position to maintain. A successfully concluded mediation removes such risks for the trustees.

CHAPTER TEN

PRACTICAL USE OF MEDIATION FOR THE ADVISOR AND CLIENT

The Significance for Lawyers and Advisors

The key issue for the lawyer and the advisor is to harness the law of mediation in such a way to encourage the other party to mediate if that is what is deemed to be in the client interests.

Negotiation

It is worth remembering that all points in a case one has the capacity to settle it without going to Court.

There are a number of ways to settle a case:

1. You make a Without Prejudice Offer that can include a Part 36 offer
2. You telephone the opponent up and have a verbal conversation to see if you can get a deal or venture one.
3. You ask your clients to sort this out themselves.
4. You ask a mutual friend to act as a go between
5. You (as a solicitor/advisor) write a letter

TIP

Mediation can be expensive and it is worth evaluating all the costs prior to considering this step. There are two particular steps which you can take prior to mediating. You can consider having a without prejudice telephone conference with the relevant advisors and/or you can consider Without Prejudice correspondence or even open correspondence. With the context of Covid 19 (December 2020) and the current delays in some of the Courts there has never been a stronger time to consider alternative dispute resolution. Lawyers need to apply flair to resolve cases. My own view is that prior to mediating you should really look at other routes to settle. The position of Covid 19 has (temporarily we hope) changed the dynamic of in person mediating.

Acting as a lawyer can be stressful and when you are acting on a case it can sometimes serve to take a step back and ask yourself some questions:

- What is the direction of this case? As it stands how do you see the case developing? What do you think will happen?
- Is the case going to head to Court and will my client win?
- And will it work from a costs point of view?
- Have you maximised your use of Without Prejudice offers and Part 36 offers to put pressure on the other side?
- Have you focused on what is driving your client and the other side?
- What would need to happen for the case to settle on a satisfactory basis for my client?
- Irrespective of the law what are the fundamental issues in the case?
- Can the areas of conflict in the case be resolved or will it take a Judge(or a third party) to sort this out?
- Is corresponding with the other side effective? Am I exercising influence on the other side's lawyer and more relevantly the other side?

The Dangers of Not Settling

It is very easy to get sucked into a dispute and the costs to build up.

Irrespective of the rights and wrongs of the dispute, beware of building up costs and assuming that these will be recovered.

During the case of Weisz V Weisz & Ors[62] inheritance dispute, a High Court Judge struggled to comprehend the £74,000 costs accrued for the one-day hearing.

Judge Francis J gave a warning on the issue of probate costs. He claimed that treating family issues with a 'commercial' mindset could reduce the amount of money spent during legal proceedings and commented:

"The claimant's costs – and this is just for today and not the claim overall – are just over £18,000. The costs of the third and fourth defendants, who are two of the children of the deceased, are £37,880. Remarkably, I am told that the executors of the estate do not even know what their costs of today are, and I should say that if any of the lawyers in this court appear in front of me again not knowing what their costs are for the application in front of me, I will have a lot more to say about it than I have done today.

"But, if I take the executors' costs as being the same as the claimant's (and I note that the claimant has instructed – I hope I can say this without any disrespect – much less expensive solicitors than the third and fourth defendants), then that means that the overall costs of today are in the order of £74,000.

"It cannot be proportionate for so much money to be spent on this issue and it is very sad indeed that the parties have been unable to settle today's application. If this were a commercial deal rather than a family row, they would not have spent this amount of money on this litigation because it would not be commercially sensible to do so, and the only way they are going to settle this litigation – whether it be next week or some time next year – rather than fight the case, the only way they are going to do so is by standing back and taking a commercial view, on advice'."

[62] Weisz v Weisz & Ors [2019] EWHC 3101 (Fam)

Do You Really Want to Mediate?

What are the benefits of mediation to lawyers & their clients?

- Generally Effective – 80% of cases work for mediation and have a successful resolution. Contrast this to the litigation process which is unpredictable, produces winners and losers and the remedy is blunt and offers limited solutions. Per the website of Centre for Effective Dispute Resolution website, over 70% of the cases that it deals with settle. The UK National Family Mediation suggests that over 80% of their mediation cases "reach full settlement".

  Other evidence in the UK is similarly impressive. And United States research which is admittedly based on evidence a couple of decades ago, suggests that the overall success rate of mediation in the US is, or at least was some twenty years ago, around 80-85%. However, the evidence is not all one way. Evidence submitted to Sir Rupert Jackson in connection with his inquiry into legal costs, for instance, showed that 95% of personal injury cases settle without the need for formal mediation. And a US study by the Rand Corporation involving 10,000 mediations suggests that, while over 70% of cases resulted in settlement, they may not have resulted in much savings by way of costs or time. Therefore, do not view mediation as some kind of panacea.

- Informal – However this should not detract from the intensity of the process but mediation is a more relaxed forum than the Court process. Clients like it because they can resolve disputes in a way that they are familiar with, namely negotiation. Whatever the rights and wrongs of the dispute a CEO of a business are not going to like being cross-examined in a witness box and this is a way to resolve that process.

- Potentially more cost effective – Mediation will normally be more cost effective than litigation. It is efficient and can avoid the "per hour" charging structure of most professional firms. The ground covered by mediation would normally take months in a traditional negotiation.

- Offers more solutions – A court is often limited in what it can award. Mediation allows for a variety of decisions to be made. In the case of Halsey Dyson LJ observed, "We recognise that mediation has several advantages over the court process. It is usually less expensive than litigation which goes all the way to judgment. Mediation provides litigants with a wider range of solutions than those that are available in litigation: for example, an apology; an explanation; the continuation of an existing professional or business relationship perhaps on new terms; and an agreement by one party to do something without any existing legal obligation to do so."

- Retain control of the process compared to litigation where even the best cases are not certain to succeed. It is crucial element of mediation that the parties choose the agreement rather than having one imposed upon them by a judge or an arbitrator.

- Speedy – The ground covered in mediation would often have taken months in a traditional negotiation.

- It is suitable where parties need a continuing relationship. Litigation tends to exacerbate differences between parties and by the end of a case parties are unlikely to want to renew their relationship. With every day that the case moves on, the relationship between the parties gets worse and worse. A senior manager is not going to take too kindly to being cross-examined in court whatever the rights and wrongs of the dispute.

- Confidential – litigation often takes place in a public forum. Mediation is both without prejudice and confidential. In these types of disputes settlements can be re-jigged so that public acknowledgements can be made and press releases issued.

- The Court may impose cost penalties if the parties can show that they have not considered mediation. Whilst this is applicable within general litigation proceedings, this does not yet apply within Employment legal proceedings though it looks likely that the new employment rules will require some form of incentive to consider mediation.

- Enforceable – A settlement contract within mediation can be enforced like any other contract though it may not be as readily enforceable as a judgement of the court.

Virtual Mediations?

Many mediations have still happened thanks to video conferencing tools, such as Zoom, Skype, FaceTime and MS Teams. Using these apps, the virtual process follows a similar pattern to conventional face-to-face mediation. Likewise, virtual shuttle mediation can still happen, by creating break out rooms using assorted types of software.

As a lawyer you should consider these as an option:

Save time and money -- A considerable cost saving can be made for a client. With no travel costs and hotel bills to pay, clients can save significant amounts of money. Mediations can sometimes be very expensive and these "hidden costs" can mount up A virtual mediation is even more cost effective and that can only be beneficial for clients albeit in person is still easier for the mediator to see.

TIP

Lawyer Mindset & Their Client Willingness to Settle is Critical Variable In Enabling Cases to Settle From direct experience the approach of lawyers (irrespective of whether you mediate or not) heavily influences the outcome.

What are the dangers of mediation and when should you not mediate?

- Need injunctive remedy – When rapid protective action is required to protect assets, evidence or reputation such as abuse of intellectual property rights.

- If you are convinced that you will do better with Court. Court cases do fundamentally involve a significant level of risk but if as a professional advisor you are convinced that you will do better in Court, then you should avoid mediation, subject to the rules of the Court.

- If you are searching for a legal precedent – For example a public judgement or an important clause in an international franchise contract or a ground-breaking employment case.

- If you have no confidence that the other party would honour the terms of the agreement. In these circumstances your party's best interests will be served by going directly towards trial and a court judgment.

- Limitation period – Formal legal proceedings need to be issued prior to expiry of limitation period although parties can consider an agreement to extend the period or an agreement to mediate in parallel with formal proceedings

- If your client really wants his or her day in Court (Though you may have to explain your client's actions if the matter does go to Court).

- If you believe that getting judicial input is the best way to go.

- The Negotiator's Dilemma – open dialogue may tempt the other side to greater demands. This is a particular dilemma relating to mediation. Nevertheless with the way that the Courts are operating it is increasingly not a sign of weakness to propose mediation.

- The other side may be on a fishing expedition though the mediator can test this.

- The other side may get a particular idea on a line on enquiry for how to pursue a case from a particular exchange that takes place in the case. Said against that, the mediator should be able to control this line of conduct. In my experience this only happens in a minority of cases.

- If there is in fact no bona fide dispute, one party's position is devoid of any merit.

- The advantage of delay heavily favours one side and it is not your client.

- There has not been sufficient disclosure or expert evidence is required before the decision to mediate can be taken.

TIP

Much of the probate work I do involves dealing with alleged probate and LPA fraud. In these circumstances I would be reluctant to mediate as trust is so much damaged between the parties.

How do you go about arranging mediation?

You can go via a mediation service provider.

The advantage of using a service provider is that for a global fee they will supply an accredited mediator, locate and hire the venue and the management of the process. The disadvantage is that the service provider may try to steer you to a particular mediator who you do not necessarily want.

Alternatively you can instruct a mediator yourself. Increasingly there are increasingly solicitors offering the service as being a mediator.

Pre-Mediation Preparation

If you wish to have mediation you need to consider some of these variables:

- Think about what point in a case you should mediate? Advantages of early mediation – before either party becomes too settled and costs have been minimised. Later case – the trial is about to take place the parties may feel that they have nothing to lose and relationship is so damaged you must mediate after a level of work has been done. It matters not whether parties have reached disclosure, witness statements but you must be comfortable with your knowledge of the case.

TIP

On any kind of conflict case you should be evaluating whether the case is ripe for settlement including mediation or not. Sometimes if you have a litigation case which has been going on a while it is good to telephone the client, explain what the legal position is, the level of costs incurred, to be incurred and then ask if the client can see if there is any way the case can be settled.

- The size of your mediation team. Leaner & smaller teams work – From the mediator's perspective a smaller team containing the person with the authority to settle is far more efficient than a larger one. The real danger of having a larger team is that everyone wants to get their six pence in. The process will be significantly weakened if you do not have the person with the authority to settle. The general principle is that the commercial decision makers are critical to the success of the mediation and accordingly it is my strong preference to have the person with authority to settle at the mediation.

- Make the right kind of preparation. Whilst it is correct that lawyers should focus on the law, ensure that you focus on the fact that this is a form of negotiation. Try to think beyond the law to see if there can be any commercial solutions, which can be of use to all the parties. In particular preparation is important at the opening statement and deciding what content should be in. You should be thinking about what your concessions will be.

- Selection of a mediator – You need to look at the professional background, the subject matter expertise, and the mediator personality – There are a variety of attributes that should be considered such as the diplomatic approach, intellectual rigour, the integrity, the patience and the persistence of the mediator. Track record – This is another variable, which needs to be considered. ADR Organisation – There are a number of ADR organisations, which exist including CEDR, The Academy of Experts and the ADR Group. These can provide support in order to assist in the selection of the mediator. The selection of the mediator is critical in determining whether the mediation will be successful. As a consequence investment in researching this will be critical.

- Anticipation of the other side. One of the dilemmas to consider is how entrenched the other side is and how they will adjust their position.

TIP

Selection of mediator is one the most important dynamics in the mediation process. A good mediator will get a case settled but a great mediator can get any case settled. Do not be seduced by mediation providers who say that this person is excellent or others such as opposing solicitors, your own counsel or your opponents. If you have a good mediator who can get the job done, try to ensure that mediator is going to be used. Typically what happens you horse trade with the other side to agree a mediator by say disclosing three mediators each. Do what you can to get a good mediator. This area of preparation can be pivotal.

- The length of the mediation. Even the most complex cases can be settled within less than 2 days. My preference is that the shortest mediation should be is 3 hours. Generally, a mediation (unless complex) should not last more than one day though it can go on late beyond office hours! It is possible that some elderly client issues can take three hours but particularly on long standing issues you are looking at one day.

- The venue. The venue is important but does not have to be at a neutral venue. By way of example there may be benefit in locating it at where the project has taken place. This will assist with site visits, access to local managers, access to relevant decision makers if need be. It is my preference that the mediation is held at a quality venue and this can have a bearing on whether the case can be settled. The slight disadvantage of holding the mediation at one of the lawyer's own premises. If the home party has a better room, this is bound to antagonise the other side. Also you need to consider if the venue for a total fee or are there extras to consider. In a two party mediation a minimum of 3 rooms are usually required. One must be large enough for all the participants and two for private sessions. The key is that your client is comfortable with the venue.

- Authority to settle. It is an essential requirement of the process that all sides come to the mediation with authority to settle. All persons who approve the settlement should attend the mediation so that they can see the dynamic, which effectively brings the settlement into play.

- You need to have an agreement to mediate. This will contain the following provisions that the proceedings are confidential and without prejudice, no party may call the mediator to give evidence in later proceedings in what he has learnt in the course of the proceedings, the process is voluntary: any party can call a halt to proceedings. This should be signed by both parties prior to the mediation taking place. A sample one is provided in the back of the book.

Dealing with The Client

Prior to the mediation taking place you should emphasise the following points to the client:

- It is likely that your client will not have the correct perception of the mediation. The mediation is NOT about the imposition of a decision by a 3rd party.
- You need to emphasise the without prejudice nature of the proceedings. The fact that the mediation is confidential and that the information exchanged obtained in the course of mediation may not be used elsewhere.[63]
- The process is consensual namely that your client is free to leave the mediation at any time.
- Once a settlement has been agreed, it becomes enforceable as a matter of contract, and as long as it is workable, it is enforceable.

[63] Venture Investment Placement Ltd v Hall 2005 EWHC 1227 (Ch) and Reed Executive Plc v Reed Business Information (2004) EWCA Civ 887 2004 1WLR 3026

Position Statements on The Day

TIP

Some mediators and indeed lawyers (particularly barristers) get in a state about having to produce a position statement. Remember you are not going to Court, you are trying to reach a deal. Also, do not neglect who is going to receive the opening statement. Its goal is to help the mediator clarify the issue and also impact the other side. That will not be achieved by trashing the other side or go into over-intelligent legal lease unless case law is really critical in the case.

In an ideal world, you should have a pre-mediation conference to consider the case with the client, counsel and relevant attendees.

With respect to their position statements, whilst knowledge of law is essential, the parties should ensure that their Statement of Cases should cover the following issues:

- Identify the parties – The mediator does not know who everyone is so prior to the mediation identify the parties to help the mediator in this regard.
- Relevant history.
- Outline of the dispute.
- Your client's case.
- The path to settlement.

The general principle with the position statement as with the bundle is that less is more. Also do not neglect to focus on a solution.

Common Failings of Lawyers During Mediation

1. Lack of Confidence in the Process – There are many lawyers who lack confidence, understanding of the process and accordingly allow this to cloud their thinking.

2. Preparing For the Case as though it was trial where you have to prove your case to a 3rd party. Linked with this, a common failing which I experience with lawyers is the tendency to be over-aggressive and making direct attacks on the other side.

3. Bringing in difficult persons who undermine the prospects of a settlement being reached.

4. Bringing in the wrong person such as someone with inadequate knowledge of the dispute.

Mediator's Functions

The mediator's role is to act as a catalyst to enable the parties to resolve the difficulty for themselves. To do this the mediator will:

- Establish exactly what the dispute is about.

- Clarify the positions of the parties and translate them into terms that are clearly understood by the parties.

- Establish what is important and what is not to each of the parties, give priorities to these various requirements.

- Establish areas of overlap and help each side to a position of compromise.

- Extend discussions into matters or proposals not previously considered.

- Make suggestions to each party concerning alternative solutions.

- Exert pressure for a solution to be reached and seek a face-saving formula where appropriate.

Overall the mediator cannot and should not take responsibility for settlement. The most important goal for the mediator is to ensure that the parties are given every opportunity to confront their differences, understand them and try to resolve them. He or she will try to break down barriers.

TIP

Fundamentally, the initial objective of the mediator is to understand what the dispute is all about, identify issues and then focus on strengths and weaknesses. Some mediators may try to apply pressure to help reach a solution. It is important that you and your client do not feel railroaded or bullied. You have the right to walk away if you want to.

Lawyer Tips for Preparation On The Day

- Do not be over-macho in opening statement- When you make an opening statement which is going to be heard from the other side, do not necessarily be over-aggressive as you may want to consider how this will be received from the other side.

- Be prepared on legal costs – A mediator may very well wish to probe you on the level of legal costs so be ready to deal with this.

- Distinguish between wants & needs – I may want a luxury performance car such as a Ferrari but I may need a car which gets me from A to B.

- Consider consequences of a failed mediation – No matter how good your mediator is, there is always a risk that the mediation will fail. Think what would happen if the case did not settle.

- Assess Strengths & Weaknesses – If there are strengths & weaknesses in your position, acknowledge them now. In the private sessions the mediator is more likely to probe you on the weaknesses so be ready here.

- Prepare during the private sessions – When the mediator is engaged in the private session with the other party ensure that you are still preparing on the case and being ready with your next move.

- The importance of signing on the day, who drafts the agreement & how is it enforced. In my experience it is much better to get the deal signed there and then whilst you have the momentum of the mediation going with you.

How to Negotiate Effectively

Since the 1970s American academics have been studying the profiles of experienced negotiators describing them as "co-operative" or "aggressive" and attempting to establish how effective which actual form of negotiation is.

The results of the research concluded that up to 87% of negotiators performed more effectively when they were co-operative. Of those who were considered to be aggressive negotiators 85% were found to be ineffective or average in terms of results achieved and only 15% effective.

Professor Gerald Williams of Brigham Young, University, Utah, USA analysed the objectives and traits of effective and ineffective negotiators and gave the following observations:

Effective Co-operative & Aggressive Negotiators

Positive traits of both:

Well prepared, realistic, self-controlled, convincing, perceptive at reading clues.

Ineffective traits include:

- Co-operative – Wishes to maintain good relations with opponent in order to get a deal which meets client's needs. He will be pressed to give away more and more without securing any advantage in return.

- Aggressive – He can be intolerant of and hostile to needs of others, and his bullying approach will lead to collapse of negotiations, which will drive the other side away from the bargaining table.

The Mediation Day & The Mediator's Techniques

The Mediation Day

As mediator there will be a number of things which I will do at the beginning of the day. I will introduce myself to the parties tend call them together.

I will then give an opening statement where I give my name, outline my experience in the law & mediation, get the parties to introduce themselves, ask if they have authority to settle, explain the process and remind them that they are free to leave at any time.

After each party has spoken, I will deal with them in private session.

The so-called plenary session provides a platform for each party to make out their case – Each party can hear the others case.

Closed Sessions

The private or closes session is a central feature of the mediation process and is the most effective dynamic of the mediation process. Here the mediator holds a series of separate meetings with the parties in the dispute. The goal of the mediator is to bring the parties together by finding hidden agenda and exploring means of reaching agreement.

The mediator will take a series of steps to emphasise confidence in the process by:

- Securing confidence – The mediator must ensure that all confidences are strictly preserved. Trust will be lost if it is suspected that even a hint of anything to the other side is being expressed to the other side.

- Clarifying issues – One of the key roles of the mediator is to see what issues actually divide the parties and see what matters they can agree on. Once these have been identified it is possible to build the items, which can be agreed upon, and to explore solutions for possible agreement.

- Avoiding value judgments – In contrast to some other forms of ADR, the mediator is not there to impose a solution and should not be judging your conduct.

- Testing reality – The mediator should examine critically the arguments that each party has put forward and probe the confidence upon which those views are held. A mediator should expose any weakness as soon as possible.

- Deflating extreme positions – Parties can take unreasonable positions and be blind to the fact that they are doing so. A Mediator can be of assistance in exposing this and then enabling face saving formulae to take place.

- Encouraging ideas between the parties – This is where a mediator can be of real assistance to the parties.

To be effective the Mediator must gain and retain the confidence and respect of the parties. Trust has to be established from the outset if the parties are to deal frankly and openly with the Mediator.

Always remembering that the Mediator is not a judge and does not have to decide between the parties' cases.

MORE BOOKS BY LAW BRIEF PUBLISHING

A selection of our other titles available now:-

- 'A Practical Guide to Solicitor and Client Costs – 2nd Edition' by Robin Dunne
- 'Constructive Dismissal – Practice Pointers and Principles' by Benjimin Burgher
- 'A Practical Guide to Religion and Belief Discrimination Claims in the Workplace' by Kashif Ali
- 'A Practical Guide to the Law of Medical Treatment Decisions' by Ben Troke
- 'Fundamental Dishonesty and QOCS in Personal Injury Proceedings: Law and Practice' by Jake Rowley
- 'A Practical Guide to the Law in Relation to School Exclusions' by Charlotte Hadfield & Alice de Coverley
- 'A Practical Guide to Divorce for the Silver Separators' by Karin Walker
- 'The Right to be Forgotten – The Law and Practical Issues' by Melissa Stock
- 'A Practical Guide to Planning Law and Rights of Way in National Parks, the Broads and AONBs' by James Maurici QC, James Neill et al
- 'A Practical Guide to Election Law' by Tom Tabori
- 'A Practical Guide to the Law in Relation to Surrogacy' by Andrew Powell
- 'A Practical Guide to Claims Arising from Fatal Accidents – 2nd Edition' by James Patience
- 'A Practical Guide to the Ownership of Employee Inventions – From Entitlement to Compensation' by James Tumbridge & Ashley Roughton
- 'A Practical Guide to Asbestos Claims' by Jonathan Owen & Gareth McAloon
- 'A Practical Guide to Stamp Duty Land Tax in England and Northern Ireland' by Suzanne O'Hara
- 'A Practical Guide to the Law of Farming Partnerships' by Philip Whitcomb

'Covid-19, Homeworking and the Law – The Essential Guide to Employment and GDPR Issues' by Forbes Solicitors

'Covid-19, Force Majeure and Frustration of Contracts – The Essential Guide' by Keith Markham

'Covid-19 and Criminal Law – The Essential Guide' by Ramya Nagesh

'Covid-19 and Family Law in England and Wales – The Essential Guide' by Safda Mahmood

'A Practical Guide to the Law of Unlawful Eviction and Harassment – 2nd Edition' by Stephanie Lovegrove

'Covid-19, Residential Property, Equity Release and Enfranchisement – The Essential Guide' by Paul Sams and Louise Uphill

'Covid-19, Brexit and the Law of Commercial Leases – The Essential Guide' by Mark Shelton

'A Practical Guide to Costs in Personal Injury Claims – 2nd Edition' by Matthew Hoe

'A Practical Guide to the General Data Protection Regulation (GDPR) – 2nd Edition' by Keith Markham

'Ellis on Credit Hire – Sixth Edition' by Aidan Ellis & Tim Kevan

'A Practical Guide to Working with Litigants in Person and McKenzie Friends in Family Cases' by Stuart Barlow

'Protecting Unregistered Brands: A Practical Guide to the Law of Passing Off' by Lorna Brazell

'A Practical Guide to Secondary Liability and Joint Enterprise Post-Jogee' by Joanne Cecil & James Mehigan

'A Practical Guide to the Pre-Action RTA Claims Protocol for Personal Injury Lawyers' by Antonia Ford

'A Practical Guide to Neighbour Disputes and the Law' by Alexander Walsh

'A Practical Guide to Forfeiture of Leases' by Mark Shelton

'A Practical Guide to Coercive Control for Legal Practitioners and Victims' by Rachel Horman

'A Practical Guide to Rights Over Airspace and Subsoil' by Daniel Gatty
'Tackling Disclosure in the Criminal Courts – A Practitioner's Guide' by Narita Bahra QC & Don Ramble
'A Practical Guide to the Law of Driverless Cars – Second Edition' by Alex Glassbrook, Emma Northey & Scarlett Milligan
'A Practical Guide to TOLATA Claims' by Greg Williams
'Artificial Intelligence – The Practical Legal Issues' by John Buyers
'A Practical Guide to the Law of Prescription in Scotland' by Andrew Foyle
'A Practical Guide to the Construction and Rectification of Wills and Trust Instruments' by Edward Hewitt
'A Practical Guide to the Law of Bullying and Harassment in the Workplace' by Philip Hyland
'How to Be a Freelance Solicitor: A Practical Guide to the SRA-Regulated Freelance Solicitor Model' by Paul Bennett
'A Practical Guide to Prison Injury Claims' by Malcolm Johnson
'A Practical Guide to the Small Claims Track' by Dominic Bright
'A Practical Guide to Advising Clients at the Police Station' by Colin Stephen McKeown-Beaumont
'A Practical Guide to Antisocial Behaviour Injunctions' by Iain Wightwick
'Practical Mediation: A Guide for Mediators, Advocates, Advisers, Lawyers, and Students in Civil, Commercial, Business, Property, Workplace, and Employment Cases' by Jonathan Dingle with John Sephton
'The Mini-Pupillage Workbook' by David Boyle
'A Practical Guide to Crofting Law' by Brian Inkster
'A Practical Guide to Spousal Maintenance' by Liz Cowell
'A Practical Guide to the Law of Domain Names and Cybersquatting' by Andrew Clemson
'A Practical Guide to the Law of Gender Pay Gap Reporting' by Harini Iyengar

'A Practical Guide to the Rights of Grandparents in Children Proceedings' by Stuart Barlow
'NHS Whistleblowing and the Law' by Joseph England
'Employment Law and the Gig Economy' by Nigel Mackay & Annie Powell
'A Practical Guide to Noise Induced Hearing Loss (NIHL) Claims' by Andrew Mckie, Ian Skeate, Gareth McAloon
'An Introduction to Beauty Negligence Claims – A Practical Guide for the Personal Injury Practitioner' by Greg Almond
'Intercompany Agreements for Transfer Pricing Compliance' by Paul Sutton
'Zen and the Art of Mediation' by Martin Plowman
'A Practical Guide to the SRA Principles, Individual and Law Firm Codes of Conduct 2019 – What Every Law Firm Needs to Know' by Paul Bennett
'A Practical Guide to Adoption for Family Lawyers' by Graham Pegg
'A Practical Guide to Industrial Disease Claims' by Andrew Mckie & Ian Skeate
'A Practical Guide to Redundancy' by Philip Hyland
'A Practical Guide to Vicarious Liability' by Mariel Irvine
'A Practical Guide to Applications for Landlord's Consent and Variation of Leases' by Mark Shelton
'A Practical Guide to Relief from Sanctions Post-Mitchell and Denton' by Peter Causton
'A Practical Guide to Equity Release for Advisors' by Paul Sams
'A Practical Guide to the Law Relating to Food' by Ian Thomas
'A Practical Guide to Financial Services Claims' by Chris Hegarty
'The Law of Houses in Multiple Occupation: A Practical Guide to HMO Proceedings' by Julian Hunt
'A Practical Guide to Unlawful Eviction and Harassment' by Stephanie Lovegrove
'Occupiers, Highways and Defective Premises Claims: A Practical Guide Post-Jackson – 2nd Edition' by Andrew Mckie

www.ingramcontent.com/pod-product-compliance
Lightning Source LLC
LaVergne TN
LVHW052322200926
848481LV00002B/637